Past Masters

General Editor Keith Thomas

Paul

E. P. Sanders is Arts and Sciences Professor of Religion at Duke University. He was formerly Dean Ireland's Professor of Exegesis in the University of Oxford and Fellow of The Queen's College. His books include *Paul and Palestinian Judaism* (1977), *Paul, the Law, and the Jewish People* (1983), and *Jesus and Judaism* (1985).

Past Masters

Forthcoming

E. P. Sanders

Paul

Oxford New York
OXFORD UNIVERSITY PRESS
1991

Oxford University Press, Walton Street, Oxford OX2 6DP

Oxford New York Toronto
Delhi Bombay Calcutta Madras Karachi
Petaling Jaya Singapore Hong Kong Tokyo
Nairobi Dar es Salaam Cape Town
Melbourne Auckland

and associated companies in
Berlin Ibadan

Oxford is a trade mark of Oxford University Press

British Library Cataloguing in Publication Data
Sanders, E. P. (Ed Parish) 1937–
Paul.
1. Paul, the Apostle, Saint
I. Title   II. Series
226.6092
ISBN 0-19-287679-1

Library of Congress Cataloging in Publication Data
Sanders, E. P.
Paul/E. P. Sanders.
p. cm.   Includes bibliographical references and index.
1. Bible.   N.T.   Epistles of Paul—Theology.   2. Paul, the Apostle,
Saint.   I. Title.
225.9'2—dc20   BS2651.S23 1991   [B]   90-39585
ISBN 0-19-287679-1

Typeset by Graphicraft Typesetters Ltd.
Printed in Great Britain by
Biddles Ltd.
Guildford and King's Lynn

Contents

1 Paul's mission

Early in the sixth decade of the Common Era, Paul, an itinerant missionary of the Christian movement, was in Corinth, mapping out his own contribution to what he saw as the last stage of God's plan for humanity. He looked simultaneously east and west. He wanted to press on to Spain, to preach the gospel where it had not yet been preached, but first he had a crucial mission to fulfil to the East: he was to take an offering from his Gentile churches, as well as representative Gentile converts, to Jerusalem (Rom. 15: 23–9; for the travelling companions, see 2 Cor. 8: 16–24). While preparing for his journey, and waiting for his ship, he wrote ahead to a way-station *en route* to Spain: the church at Rome. He intended to prepare them for his arrival by sharing with them his message, and he also asked for their support—both their prayers that his trip to Jerusalem would be successful and aid, probably monetary, for the trip to Spain (Rom. 1: 11–15; 15: 24; 15: 30 f.).

His mind, however, was still filled with conflicts that lay behind him, casting their shadow over his trip to Jerusalem—a trip that filled him with apprehension. He asked the Romans to pray that he would be 'delivered from the unbelievers' and also that his service for Jerusalem would be 'acceptable to the saints'. That is, he anticipated danger from non-Christian Jews, and he feared rejection by the Jewish members of the Christian movement. His career up to then had been full of contention, including confrontation with prominent followers of Jesus in Jerusalem. As he thought about meeting the Jerusalem disciples, he rethought his past conflicts, and he considered how he could best state his case. Since his career in Asia Minor and Greece was over, he also paused to reflect on the overall progress of the Christian gospel, and he speculated on how it would all turn out.

He wrote all this up: both his argument against other

Christian leaders on disputed issues (the continuing validity of the Jewish law; the place of Gentiles in God's plan; the maintenance of high standards of behaviour if the law were given up) and an exposition of the divine plan itself, of God's intention for both Jews and Greeks, and of his own role in that plan. He sent what he wrote as an introductory letter to Rome. The letter eventually became one of the most influential documents of western history, the Epistle to the Romans. It began, however, as a quite particular letter, set in an identifiable context, and discussing concrete problems and plans.

We learn, first, who Paul thought he was. This is absolutely crucial for understanding the controversies of his letters, and it is also the easiest point of entry for understanding his theology: his theology was bound up with a view of himself and his role in God's plan; it was not, perhaps, determined entirely by his self-perception, but certainly not separable from it.

Who was he? He was the one who would fulfil the expectations of the prophets and perhaps of Jesus himself: he would bring the Gentiles to worship the God of Israel. This assertion, which appears several times in the letter, is emphasized at the beginning and the end, where it would make most impact:

[I] have received grace and apostleship to bring about the obedience of faith ... among all the Gentiles, including yourselves. (Rom. 1: 5f.)

I have often intended to come to you ... in order that I may reap some harvest among you as well as among the rest of the Gentiles. I am under obligation both to Greeks and to barbarians [that is, to all Gentiles], both to the wise and to the foolish: so I am eager to preach the gospel to you also who are in Rome. (1: 13–15)

Now I am speaking to you Gentiles: Since I am apostle to the Gentiles ... (11: 13)

In chapter 15 the point of Paul's definition of his role becomes clearer. He writes that Christ himself was 'a servant to the circumcised' partly to redeem God's promises to the patriarchs, but partly in order to bring the Gentiles to glorify the God of Israel (15: 8f.). He, Paul, is the one who is seeing to this. He is 'a minister of Christ Jesus to the Gentiles', carrying out 'a priestly ministry' in the service of the gospel of God, in order that 'the offering of the Gentiles might be acceptable' (15: 16). Only about this will he speak: what God has done through him 'to win obedience from the Gentiles' (15: 18).

These verses in Romans 15 show not only that Paul thought of himself as emissary to the Gentiles, but that he thought of himself in this way within a given context: a context both in history and, more important, in God's plan. God planned it in advance: he sent his Son partly in order to bring in the Gentiles. In converting Gentiles, Paul had been fulfilling a 'priestly' ministry, and he was now bringing them as an 'offering' to Jerusalem, where the temple was. We know from what world view, or view of saving history, that comes. It is the long-held Jewish expectation that, in the final days, Gentiles would come to worship the God of Israel. They would come to Mount Zion bearing gifts, or offerings, and they would come bringing themselves to serve God. This is the second half of a standard Jewish expectation about the end: God would first restore Israel, and then Gentiles would come in. In chapter 15 Paul quotes a catena of passages from the Jewish Scripture which express the hope that the Gentiles will come to worship the God of Israel. Paul saw himself as the agent of this, the second half of the divine plan. His job description was this: Apostle to the Gentiles in the Messianic Era.

To bring into full relief how he saw his task, we must note how he depicted his responsibility for Israel, the way in which he saw his mission as contributing to the first half of the overall plan. Peter and others were responsible for persuading Jews to be disciples of Jesus (Gal. 2: 7), but they had not been very successful. Paul saw his own work among Gentiles as contributing only indirectly to the winning of Jews. He 'glorified' his own service as apostle to the Gentiles, 'so that, perhaps, I may make jealous my kin, and I shall save some of them' (Rom. 11: 13 f.). The theme that Israel would be brought to Christ indirectly, after the Gentile mission and because of it, appears twice more in Romans 11, in verses 25–6 and 30–1. This reversal of sequence—first the Gentiles rather than first the Jews—will occupy us later, in Chapter 11, and here it need be noted only that Paul saw his own role in the light of biblical promises about

3

the entry of the Gentiles into the people of God in 'the last days'.

The last days were at hand: God's plan was nearing completion, despite the Jewish rejection of Jesus as Messiah. Time was so short that Paul felt that he must hurry. He considered that the few churches which he had established in Asia Minor, Macedonia and Greece left him no 'room for work in these regions', and he thought that, in his ministry of about twenty years, he had 'completed' the gospel 'from Jerusalem and in a circle as far as Illyricum' (Rom. 15: 19; the Revised Standard Version, rather misleadingly, has 'fully preached' for 'completed'). He may have thought that the churches that he had founded would produce evangelists who would expand the Christian mission into the hinterland (as Epaphras seems to have done in Colossae, Col. 1: 7), and certainly there were in Asia Minor and Greece many missionaries who were independent of Paul. We occasionally meet them in his letters. Apollos was not under Paul's control (see 1 Cor. 1: 12 and 16: 12); Andronicus and Junia, apparently a missionary couple, were independent of him (Rom. 16: 7); another couple, Prisca and Aquila, seem to have worked on their own, though sometimes in collaboration with Paul (Rom. 16: 3; Acts 18: 2); and doubtless there were many others. Thus Paul may have begun to feel a little crowded. Still, the desire to hasten on to Spain also reflects his commitment to finish the task before the Lord returned.

Though in Romans 15: 19 Paul speaks of 'completing' the gospel in a 'circle', we know from the subsequent verses that, even in his own view, he had not truly finished, since he was still planning to go on to Spain. Further, the arc which he saw himself as following (from the centre of the eastern edge of the Mediterranean, curving north-west, continuing west, and curving south-west to Spain) did not seem destined to make a complete circle. It is a curious fact that in the New Testament there is no mention of a plan to evangelize North Africa, even though it was populous and had very important centres of Jewish settlement, especially in Egypt and Cyrenaica. Perhaps there was such a plan and Paul just does not mention it. To this day we do not know how or when the Christian message was

4

brought to Alexandria, which suddenly emerged at the end of the second century as one of the major centres of Christianity. In any case, we see throughout Paul's letters, and especially in Romans, the urgency he felt: God would not long delay. It was up to Paul and the others to cover the ground quickly, since the night was far gone, and the day at hand; full salvation was perceptibly nearer than when the Romans first came to faith (Rom. 13: 11 f.).

But, despite the inevitable working of the plan of God, it was to take place in human history, and humans are notoriously cantankerous and frequently unwilling to fit into a grand scheme. We have already seen that when Paul wrote the letter he was very worried about the forthcoming trip to Jerusalem. It was possible that without the Romans' prayers he would not be able to come to them with joy (15: 30-2); either the 'unbelievers' might harm him, or the 'saints' might reject his service.

He had good reason for both worries. He had already had trouble from both non-Christian Jews and Jewish Christians, as well as from non-Christian Gentiles. Not long before writing Romans, Paul had compared himself with other missionaries and had claimed that he had served Christ with

far greater labours, far more imprisonments, with countless beatings, and often near death. Five times I have received at the hands of the Jews the forty lashes less one. Three times I have been beaten with rods; once I was stoned. Three times I have been shipwrecked; a night and a day I have been adrift at sea; on frequent journeys, in danger from rivers, danger from robbers, danger from my own people, danger from Gentiles, danger in the city, danger in the wilderness, danger from false brethren; in toil and hardship, through many a sleepless night, in hunger and thirst, often without food, in cold and exposure. (2 Cor. 11: 23-7)

This includes every place as a source of danger and every group—except for Pauline Christians—as among Paul's enemies. The punishment of 'forty lashes less one' was the official synagogue punishment; that of being beaten with rods was the simplest punishment at the disposal of Roman magistrates; stoning was the action of an angry mob. We may sometimes suspect

Paul of rhetorical exaggeration. 'Countless beatings' is an instance: he promptly counts them. We can, however, accept the count as accurate.

Shortly after writing the passage just quoted (in a passage which the first editor of Paul's correspondence placed earlier), Paul returned to his sufferings and difficulties: he had been 'afflicted in every way, but not crushed ... persecuted, but not forsaken; struck down, but not destroyed'. Yet he counted these things to be an intrinsic part of his participation in Christ: 'While we live we are always being given up to death for Jesus' sake, so that the life of Jesus may be manifested in our bodies' (2 Cor. 4: 8–11). Paul did not have a martyr complex. While he did not seek suffering, he endured it because he counted 'the sufferings of this present time' not to be worth comparing 'with the glory that is to be revealed to us' (Rom. 8: 18).

The 'false brethren' constituted a serious problem, and danger from them probably worried him more than the punishments administered by synagogues and Roman magistrates. They were 'brethren' because they believed that Jesus was the Messiah (in Pauline terms, they had faith in Christ); they were 'false' because of what they taught. When, in Romans 15: 30, Paul asked the Romans to 'wrestle' with him in prayer, so that his service might be 'acceptable to the saints', he was really asking the Romans to pray that the members of the Jerusalem church would not be persuaded by the 'false brethren', but rather by him, and that they would agree that what he had been doing was right and that his converts were counted as belonging to 'the household of faith'.

The problem was that some Christian missionaries, and possibly some of the Jerusalem leadership, did not agree that Paul's mission was valid. There were some who preached 'a different gospel', or a gospel contrary to Paul's (Gal. 1: 8f.; 2 Cor. 11: 4). These were worse than people who simply meted out physical punishment. Paul hurled a curse against those who preached a different gospel to the Galatians (Gal. 1: 8f.), and he went on to wish that they would physically mutilate themselves (Gal. 5: 12). If the Galatians followed them, he said, they would be severed from Christ (Gal. 5: 4). His opponents in Corinth, who obviously were generally counted as apostles of Christ, he called 'false apostles, deceitful workmen, disguising themselves as apostles of Christ', and finally 'servants of Satan'. Their end, he said, would correspond to their deeds (2 Cor. 11: 13–15).

This is a strange situation for one who counted his ministry a success, who could boast about his Gentile converts, who saw them as instrumental in bringing about the redemption of Israel, and who saw his endeavour in Asia Minor and Greece as being so successful that he no longer had 'any room for work in these regions' (Rom. 15: 23). What was the trouble? What did Paul do that created enemies in every quarter, including within the Christian movement? How did he get into the position of regarding his work as successful, but of fearing that it might not be acceptable?

This question starts two lines of enquiry. One is the analysis of Paul's gospel, especially as it stood over against that of others. This leads us into the major theological parts of his work: the argument about 'righteousness by faith and not by law'; the meaning of 'life in Christ Jesus'; and so on. We need also, however, to study his career more generally, in order to understand his role in the Christian movement and the curious combination of feeling both successful and on the brink of failure. We shall take the biographical route first, following it long enough to say something about his activities and personal characteristics, before we turn to his thought, which has been the source of controversy from his day to ours.

2 Paul's life

Paul was a Jew from Tarsus, a city near the south-east corner of Asia Minor. The date of his birth is unknown, but he was probably born about the same time as Jesus. The years during which he accomplished deeds that would indelibly write his name in history were approximately 36–60 CE. Most scholars put his death in Rome in the year 62 or 64.

For roughly the first half of his life he was a Pharisee. Very little is known about Paul the Pharisee except that, on his own estimation, he was a very good one (as we shall see below). We know little about what a Greek-speaking Pharisee in Asia Minor would have been. Pharisees believed in the resurrection, as did Paul (1 Cor. 15). Pharisees also observed 'traditions' above and beyond the written law, and Paul explicitly mentions that he was extremely zealous for the traditions of his fathers (Gal. 1: 14). But just what the traditions were, in his time and place, is not certain. According to Acts 22: 3, Paul had studied under the leading Pharisee of his day, Gamaliel I, but this may be no more than an inference drawn by the author of Acts from the fact that Paul was an outstanding Pharisee and that Gamaliel was the leader of the party. We shall see below that there are reasons to doubt Paul's residence as a youth and young man in Jerusalem.

The one activity which can be ascribed to Paul the Pharisee with certainty is his persecution of the Christian movement. It is important to note that this had to do with Paul's zeal, but not with his Pharisaism. Acts represents Gamaliel as speaking in favour of tolerance for the Christian movement (5: 33–9). If Paul had been a student of Gamaliel's he did not learn harshness and persecution from him. But in either case there is no reason to attribute persecution to the Pharisees or to Paul's Pharisaism. Acts, to continue with its evidence, presents the chief priests as the enemies of the movement (Acts 4: 1 and throughout), and this is confirmed by the fact that James, Jesus' brother, was executed on the orders of the Sadducaean high priest Ananas (*Jewish Antiquities* 20: 199–203). Further, according to Acts, it was the High Priest, who was a Sadducee (Acts 5: 17), who authorized Paul to go to the synagogues in Damascus and to bring back to Jerusalem Jews who had accepted Jesus (9: 1–2). It was on this trip that he was converted from persecutor to apostle (9: 3–9).

Paul's letters confirm that he was a persecutor, though they offer none of the details which are in Acts. The reader of Galatians would have to doubt that Paul was called while travelling to Damascus from Jerusalem. He writes that after his call he went into Arabia and then returned to Damascus, making it seem that he was there all along (Gal. 1: 27). Further, the account in Galatians throws doubt on the theory of Acts that Paul conducted his persecution in Jerusalem and had that city as his base. According to Galatians 1: 22 he was not known by sight to the churches in Judaea, which makes it most unlikely that Jerusalem had been the scene of his activity as persecutor. That he persecuted the Christian movement, however, is not in doubt. He says this of himself in Galatians 1: 13, 23; 1 Corinthians 15: 9; Philippians 3: 6, though details are completely missing. It may be that his early career as persecutor consisted of persuading synagogues to administer to those who accepted Jesus the severest punishment a synagogue could mete out—the thirty-nine lashes that he himself later suffered.

The change of career, from persecutor to apostle of the very movement he had been persecuting, came in about the year 33. Either on the road to Damascus (so Acts), or in Damascus (the inference from Galatians), God revealed Christ to him. Acts has Paul describe this revelation as a bright light which left him temporarily blinded (Acts 22: 6–11), but Paul himself said only that 'God revealed his Son to me' (Gal. 1: 16). Elsewhere he claimed to have seen the Risen Lord, not a bright light (1 Cor. 9: 1). He considered this to be a resurrection appearance, and it was part of his justification for considering himself equal to the original apostles (1 Cor. 9: 1; 15: 8). His call was not just to serve Christ, but to accomplish a special task: the conversion of Gentiles (Gal. 1: 16). This was then his whole activity for the next thirty or so years.

Fortunately Paul wrote letters, and equally fortunately someone collected, edited, and published some of them. In these letters a remarkable human being still speaks, and it is in them that we find Paul—a man full of flash and fire, passion and vigour, wit and charm, pride and humility, enormous self-confidence, and fear and trembling.

The letters reveal many personal traits and a fair bit about his life. Paul, destined to become Jesus' most influential spokesman, never met him, and he first met the leading disciples approximately three years after his own conversion (Gal. 1: 18). The contrast between Paul, on the one hand, and Jesus, Peter and the other Galileans, on the other, could hardly have been greater. Jesus was from a very small village; he was either a carpenter, or the son of one, or both, but in any case closer to the peasants who worked the land than to the merchants who travelled the Mediterranean; and he seems never to have travelled enough to have had the opportunity to compare different cultures and experience different societies and their values. Paul, on the other hand, was an urbanite and a cosmopolitan, moving easily throughout the Graeco-Roman world. He could probably speak Aramaic (or Hebrew, or both; Acts 21: 40), and he may have known Latin, but his main tongue was one of the greatest international languages of all time: *koine* (common) Greek.

Paul's letters show him to be a man of what we would now call middle-class upbringing. Ancient categories of status were not the same as ours, but the term 'middle class' is in many ways appropriate. His Greek is clear and forceful, but not elegant; unlike his wealthy contemporary, the Jewish philosopher Philo of Alexandria, he had not had the kind of education which led to elegant prose. Paul had learned a trade, called 'tent making' in Acts 18: 3. People who could afford to travel with their own tents were fortunate, since they could thereby avoid public inns, which were often infested with vermin, and Paul's trade probably served such people. He boasted that, as a missionary, he supported himself by working with his own hands (1 Cor. 4: 12). This is revealing: the poor do not find working with their hands to be worthy of special remark. Paul may have been trained for ownership or management. He knew how to use a secretary, and he dictated his letters (see Gal. 6: 11, where he notes when he writes in his own hand, and Romans 16: 22, where his scribe sends his own greetings). He also knew how to organize and plan. Most of the time he had more than one assistant; and he could send one here, another there, while himself going elsewhere, and rejoin them to assess the situation and make further plans.

As apostle, however, he did not live in comfortably middle-class conditions. He knew how to be abased and how to 'abound' (Phil. 4: 11–12), but his commitment to his cause often meant that materially he did not have abundance. 'To the present hour we hunger and thirst, we are ill-clad and buffeted and homeless' (1 Cor. 4: 11). He worked in circumstances which would discourage most: 'in toil and hardship, through many a sleepless night, in hunger and thirst, often without food, in cold and exposure' (2 Cor. 11: 28). This poverty, however, was voluntary, and in Paul's letters we do not hear the voice of the lowest level of Graeco-Roman society. Further, sometimes he did 'abound'. Romans 16, which may originally have been a separate letter, introduces Phoebe, whom he describes as his 'patroness' (16: 2; patroness is unhelpfully translated 'helper' by the RSV). In a personal letter to Philemon he instructs the recipient to prepare a guest room for him (Philm. 22). Thus some of the time he lived in comfort.

Paul upheld many of the standard values of his society, especially as modified by the Jewish communities. He regarded it to be against nature for men to have long hair and immodest for women to pray with heads uncovered (1 Cor. 11: 4–16), which shows that he accepted standard fashions. He appears himself to have been celibate (1 Cor. 7: 7), but he urged married partners to engage in sex regularly (1 Cor. 7: 5). He frowned on divorce, but he could tolerate it: he quotes and then modifies Jesus' prohibition (1 Cor. 7: 10–16). Unlike pagans, but like other Jews, he abhorred homosexual activity (Rom. 1: 26–7). He did not favour excessive displays of charismatic gifts (1 Cor. 13: 1–14: 19); he urged his converts to do everything 'decently and in order', so as not to make outsiders think that the Christians were mad. Only one at a time should speak in tongues or prophesy. 'God is not a God of confusion, but of peace!' (1 Cor. 14: 22–40).

Paul's theology contained the potential for social revolution. He thought that 'There is neither Jew nor Greek, there is neither slave nor free, there is neither male nor female; for you are all one in Christ Jesus' (Gal. 3: 28). Yet this was not a social programme, and the only point to which he tried to give effect was the union of Jew and Gentile. Slaves were full 'brothers' in Christ (Philm. 16), but they should not seek freedom from ownership (1 Cor. 7: 21–3). To women he accorded equality in many ways (1 Cor. 7: 4; 11: 8–12), yet he wanted the usual distinction of sexual roles to be maintained (1 Cor. 14: 33–6). 'The appointed time [had] grown short' and 'the form of this world [was] passing away' (1 Cor. 7: 29–31). There was not time to remake society.

In short, Paul combined zeal with sobriety, good judgement, and administrative skills; an innovative and challenging theology with social practicality; and religious fervour with concrete planning. He was the ideal apostle for a new religion in the Graeco-Roman world.

Though the call to be an apostle had reversed the direction of his life, Paul in many ways remained the same. Paul the apostle shared many of the characteristics of Paul the Pharisee. One of the principal ones was that he was a zealot fully and totally committed to the course to which he felt called by God. Further, in both his careers he was, by his own modest estimate, the best there was:

For you have heard of my former life in Judaism, how I persecuted the church of God violently and tried to destroy it; and I advanced in Judaism beyond many of my own age among my people, so extremely zealous was I for the traditions of my fathers. (Gal. 1: 13–15)

If any other man thinks he has reason for confidence in the flesh, I have more: circumcised on the eighth day, of the people of Israel, of the tribe

of Benjamin, a Hebrew born of Hebrews; as to the law a Pharisee, as to
zeal a persecutor of the church, as to righteousness under the law
blameless. (Phil. 3: 4–6)

Likewise, on his apostleship:

For I am the least of the apostles, unfit to be called an apostle, because
I persecuted the church of God. But by the grace of God I am what
I am, and his grace toward me was not in vain. On the contrary, I
worked harder than any of them. (1 Cor. 15: 9–10)

He added, to be sure, that 'it was not I, but the grace of God'
(cf. also Phil. 4: 13), but he thought that God had chosen at
least one of his apostles well.

When his authority was directly challenged by other apostles
in Corinth, he again asserted his status and ability:

I think that I am not in the least inferior to these superlative apostles
... But whatever any one dares to boast of—I am speaking as a fool—
I also dare to boast of that. Are they Hebrews? So am I. Are they
Israelites? So am I. Are they descendants of Abraham? So am I. Are
they servants of Christ? I am a better one! (2 Cor. 11: 5, 21–3)

Thus, as Pharisee and as apostle, Paul could say that he was
among the best, and there is no reason to doubt his word.

The Corinthian correspondence brings out another aspect of
Paul. In the midst of one of the boasts above, he said, 'even if I
am unskilled in speaking, I am not in knowledge.' (2 Cor. 11: 6).
Earlier, comparing himself with Apollos, he wrote, 'I was with
you in weakness and in much fear and trembling; and my
speech and my message were not in plausible words of wisdom'
(1 Cor. 2: 3–4). His opponents could say that 'his letters are
weighty and strong, but his bodily presence is weak, and his
speech of no account' (2 Cor. 10: 10), and he had to grant the
point. He was 'unskilled in speaking' and apparently unimpress-
ive in looks.

He countered these attacks in two ways. First he claimed that,
though he did not preach with eloquence and wisdom, as did
Apollos, he was in fact not deficient, for he spoke the 'wisdom of
God', which is foolishness to humans: 'Jesus Christ and him

crucified'; and by the Spirit he spoke 'the mind of Christ' (1 Cor. 1: 18–2: 16). His second ploy to defend himself, despite his personal deficiency, was more effective and shows even better his quickness and resourcefulness: he turned his defects into virtues, and his weakness became his strength.

If I must boast, I will boast of the things that show my weakness (2 Cor. 11: 30)

Three times I besought the Lord about this [the 'thorn in the flesh'], that it should leave me; but he said to me, 'My grace is sufficient for you, for my power is made perfect in weakness.' (2 Cor. 12: 8–9)

I will all the more gladly boast of my weaknesses, that the power of Christ may rest upon me. For the sake of Christ, then, I am content with weaknesses, insults, hardships, persecutions and calamities; for when I am weak, then I am strong. (2 Cor. 12: 9–10)

And, in this mood, he could ridicule the 'strength' of his converts:

Already you are filled! Already you have become rich! Without us you have become kings! And would that you did reign, so that we might share the rule with you! For I think that God has exhibited us apostles as last of all, like men sentenced to death; because we have become a spectacle to the world, to angels and to men ... We have become, and are now, as the refuse of the world, the offscouring of all things. (1 Cor. 3: 8–13)

Paul, we thus learn, was not only weak in bodily presence and speech, but also afflicted by a 'thorn in the flesh' (some ailment which is never specified; see 2 Corinthians 12: 7; 4: 10; Galatians 4: 13–14).

Besides the combination of pride and humility, and vigour and weakness, we see in these exchanges a good deal of mental agility as he tried to present as advantages qualities which were normally considered defects in a public figure.

We have seen that he was called to be apostle in about the year 33. Romans was written approximately twenty years later. In the interval he had steadily worked his way west from Antioch, establishing churches across Asia Minor, in Macedonia and in Greece, especially in substantial cities. When he said that he had completed the gospel, and had no further room for work in the eastern half of the Mediterranean (Rom. 15: 20, 23), he evidently was thinking representatively. He had actually established churches only in selected areas.

During the twenty-year period he had twice visited Jerusalem. Once, three years after his vision of Christ, he had gone there to 'get to know' Cephas (Peter), but he 'saw none of the other apostles except James the Lord's brother' (Gal. 1: 18–19). 'After fourteen years' (whether fourteen years after the first visit, or fourteen years after his call is uncertain) he went again, to fight out the principal theological issue of his career. He took Titus, a Gentile convert and valued assistant, who became the object of controversy (Gal. 2: 1). This brought to a head the question of whether or not Paul's Gentile converts had also to become Jewish, an issue which will occupy us in Chapters 6 and 7. Just now we note only that, before leaving Jerusalem, he struck a bargain with James, Peter, and John: he, Paul, would continue to attempt to win Gentiles and would not require them to convert to Judaism by accepting circumcision, but he would also take up a collection from his churches and bring or send the money to Jerusalem (Gal. 2: 6–10).

After coming to the agreement with the Jerusalem leaders, Paul spent most of the rest of his life taking up the collection; he delivered it himself, though he was tempted just to send it (Rom. 15: 25–9; 1 Cor. 16: 3–4). He knew that he faced danger in Jerusalem, as we saw above, but finally he put aside his fears and carried out one of his last free acts in order to show that the body of Christ was one, though its members were diverse (cf. 1 Cor. 12: 12).

We can go no further on the basis of Paul's own letters. The story is picked up by Acts. While we must often query the portrait of Paul in Acts, what happened to him after he took the offering to Jerusalem would have been well known, and Acts can be relied on with regard to the main events. The collection was accepted by James, and so Paul's worry about a rupture caused by the 'false brethren' came to nothing (Acts 21: 17–26). His other enemies, 'the unbelievers in Judea' (Rom. 15: 31), however, mounted an attack which was ultimately successful. He was accused of taking a Gentile into the temple; that is, farther in than the court of the Gentiles. This led to some tumult and consequently to intervention by Roman troops and to Paul's arrest and imprisonment in Caesarea, the coastal city where the Roman procurator of Judaea resided. He was there for a few years, finally being sent to Rome to be tried (Acts 21–8), and he was in prison in Rome for at least two years (Acts 28: 30–1). The author of Acts ends the story there. Some scholars think that Paul was eventually released and went to Spain, where he wrote 1 and 2 Timothy and Titus. These letters, however, were written by a follower after his death, and probably he was martyred in Rome. It is simplest to think that Acts ends the story because Paul's career had come to its conclusion, and the author chose not to describe what may have been a ghastly end. The first readers, on this view, knew that Paul had perished and did not need to be told.

Both opinions can appeal to 1 Clement, a letter from the Bishop of Rome to the Corinthian church in about the year 96. Of Paul he wrote this:

seven times he wore fetters, he was exiled, he was stoned, he was a herald both in the east and in the west, he gained the noble renown of his faith, he taught righteousness throughout the whole world and, having reached the limit [*terma*] of the West, he bore testimony before the rulers, and so departed from the world and was taken up into the holy place—the greatest example of endurance. (1 Clem. 5: 1–7)

The phrase '*terma* of the West', if taken to mean 'physical limit', inclines the reader to think that Paul reached Spain. If it means 'goal of the West', in the sense of 'Paul's fixed destination', then Rome will do very well. The reference to 'testimony before rulers' most naturally means those of Rome.

The implication of Acts is that Paul was in Rome for only two years. Counting from his second trial in Caesarea (Acts 24–6), and allowing for the journey to Rome, some put his death in the year 62. It is often supposed, however, that both he and Peter died in the first Roman persecution of Christians. Rome had suffered a major fire in July 64. Though Nero had been away, rumour fastened the blame for the fire on him. He needed a scapegoat, and he settled on followers of the new 'superstition'. This is the description by the Roman historian, Tacitus:

Their execution was made a matter of sport: some were sewn up in the skins of wild beasts and savaged to death by dogs; others were fastened to crosses as living torches, to serve as lights when daylight failed. Nero made his gardens available for the show and held games in the Circus, mingling with the crowd or standing in his chariot in charioteer's uniform. (*Annals* 44: 3–8)

If Paul did so end his days, the hideous suffering would not have surprised him. He expected Christians—and especially apostles—to suffer and thus become in that way too one with their Lord. And he believed that he and the others would be 'fellow heirs with Christ, provided we suffer with him in order that we may also be glorified with him' (Rom. 8: 17). Suffering, and, no doubt, death itself, he met with this confidence:

Who shall separate us from the love of Christ? Shall tribulation, or distress, or persecution, or famine, or nakedness, or peril, or sword? . . . No, in all these things we are more than conquerors through him who loved us. For I am sure that neither death, nor life, . . . nor anything else in all creation, will be able to separate us from the love of God in Christ Jesus our Lord. (Rom. 8: 35–9)

We shall see in Chapter 4 that Paul expected to be alive when the Lord returned, though sometimes he reckoned with the possibility that he would die first. In either case, he foresaw neither the centuries which lay ahead nor the role in shaping subsequent history which some of his letters would play. They were collected by a disciple, probably near the year 90. When edited and published they made an enormous impact on Christians. Just as Paul was embroiled in theological controversy when he wrote his letters, so were many of those who read them in the second and subsequent centuries. People who would later be branded 'heretical' cited him in their favour, as did the defenders of 'orthodoxy'. Dualists, who believed that the physical universe is evil and that Jesus had not been a real man, appealed to some aspects of Paul's letters. The author of the Second Epistle of Peter warned his readers not to follow 'the ignorant and unstable', who twisted Paul's words 'to their own destruction', though he granted that 'there are some things in them hard to understand' (2 Pet. 3: 16). Other Christians set about making Paul more readily comprehensible and closer to what became mainstream Christianity. Some added new letters to the Pauline collection which explicitly affirmed that Jesus Christ 'was manifested in the flesh' (1 Tim. 3: 16) and that 'everything created by God is good' (4: 4). The author of Acts portrayed Paul as being always in agreement with Peter, thus masking the sometimes fierce debate among the early apostles. Such efforts 'saved' Paul for mainstream Christianity, and his letters became a central part of the New Testament as it developed between the third and sixth centuries. His passionate embrace of faith in Christ and the force of his writing have always made him one of Christianity's foremost spokesmen and by far its most exciting and vigorous theologian—though he is still difficult to understand.

Major restatements of Christian theology have often been based on Paul's letters. This was true of Augustine in the fifth century, Martin Luther in the sixteenth, and Karl Barth in the twentieth. Since Paul was himself polemical, his letters serve well those who attack other forms of Christianity. Augustine, Luther, and Barth, to be sure, all read Paul through their own spectacles and interpreted him in ways appropriate to their own circumstances. The attempt of the present work is not to use Paul to address the present situation, but rather to try to reconstruct what he thought, and why he thought it, and to do so in the categories of his own time and place.

3 Missionary strategy and message

Strategy and technique

Acts offers two descriptions of how Paul won adherents. In one instance, in Athens, he debated with other philosophers in the public market (*agora*) (Acts 17: 17). In Athens and other cities, however, he is depicted as going first of all to the local synagogue to attempt to convince Jews that Jesus was the Messiah (Acts 9: 20; 13: 5, 14; 14: 1 and elsewhere). Both procedures were reasonable, and their reasonableness doubtless accounts for their description in Acts. Yet the author of Acts and Paul disagreed fundamentally about his mission. Acts sees Paul as first of all apostle to the Jews of the Greek-speaking Diaspora. Paul regarded himself, however, as apostle to the Gentiles. So he describes himself (see above, pp. 2–3), and accordingly he describes his converts as former pagans: the Thessalonians had turned to God from idols (1 Thess. 1: 9); the Galatians had formerly worshipped 'beings which are not gods' (Gal. 4: 8); the Corinthians had worshipped dumb idols (1 Cor. 12: 2; cf. 6: 9–11); the Philippians were not circumcised (Phil. 3: 2).

Perhaps most telling is the fact that near the end of his career, when he wrote Romans, Paul could imagine for himself only an indirect role in the redemption of Israel. The Jewish people as such hardly figure in his letters until Romans 9–11. Had he spent the previous twenty years preaching in synagogues, the letters to his own churches would reflect the effort in some way or other; there would be some remark about the former state of Jewish members of his churches or about the Jews' rejection of his message. But in fact, apart from Romans 16, we learn only about Gentile converts, and until chapters 9–11 there is no reflection on the fate of the Jewish people. It seems, then, that we must think of Paul as preaching directly to Gentiles.

How did he go about it? It may at first strike us as difficult for a wandering evangelist to stroll into a city, address himself to pagans in the name of the God of Israel, and persuade them that God had sent his Son for the salvation of all, Jew and Gentile alike. In fact this may not have been all that hard. He could have argued in the public market; and, had he been a philosopher, this is probably what he would have done. Thus when the author of Acts depicts Paul as speaking in the market square of Athens, he also describes his debating partners as Epicurean and Stoic philosophers (Acts 17: 17 f.). Religion, however, was either civic, ethnic, or personal, and religious cults were usually established by means other than philosophical debate. While Paul may sometimes have engaged in public discussions, we should be prepared to think of other methods by which he spread the gospel.

We noted above that Paul was not an eloquent speaker, and this is a further reason for doubting that he relied principally on public addresses. There is a more likely explanation. Whenever he entered a new city, he probably took a room in which to ply his trade, and he talked with whoever came in or walked past. Cutting and sewing leather (of which tents were usually made) was a fairly quiet occupation, and it would not have interfered with discussion. We cannot know for sure just how Paul reached interested hearers, and he may have employed diverse means. He was probably most effective, however, one-to-one, or in small groups.

The fact that he represented a religion from the Middle East would not have been a barrier. While the success of Asian cults in Mediterranean cities may have been overestimated in the past, they were not uncommon. Pagans knew Jews and Judaism, and some would have been interested by a new movement within it. Although Judaism was often scorned it also had its admirers. Monotheism was philosophically attractive, Judaism's high ethics appealed to many, and the sabbath rest was sometimes emulated. A spokesman for the God of Israel would have found willing hearers.

The message that Paul offered had its allure. There was only one feature which would have made its acceptance difficult:

exclusivism. We learn in 1 Corinthians that not all the converts there wanted totally to exclude participation in some of the aspects of the common paganism, and we must imagine that many more refused to join the Christian movement because Christians, like Jews generally, would not tolerate the worship of other gods by full members of their own communities.

Many, however, would have heard quite gladly the message that, by being baptized and professing faith in Christ, they would be assured of eternal life. In matters religious, the general attitude was often the more the merrier—or at least, the more the better chance—and it seems not to have been difficult to get a sizeable number of people to increase their chances of a happy future by joining religions or cults. Paul may not have emphasized at first the exclusivism which he shared with other Jews, and the opening message of Jesus' death and especially his resurrection—to which Paul could personally testify—would have captured interest.

His basic message

We know with a good deal of precision what Paul preached, at least in outline, since in his surviving letters he often recalls what he had first said. He preached the death, resurrection, and lordship of Jesus Christ, and he proclaimed that faith in him guaranteed a share in his life. This is the earliest surviving summary of a Christian sermon, written to Thessalonica in Macedonia possibly as early as 41 CE, no more than about ten years after Jesus' death.

[Others] report concerning us what a welcome we had among you, and how you turned to God from idols, to serve a living and true God, and to wait for his Son from heaven, whom he raised from the dead, Jesus who delivers us from the wrath to come. (1 Thess. 1: 9–10)

Here Paul emphasizes Jesus' resurrection and the promise that those who belonged to him would be saved from the coming 'wrath'. The promise of salvation to believers was not only important, it was urgent. Paul expected most people then living to be still alive when the Lord returned (1 Thess. 4: 14–18; see further in Chapter 4 of this book), the event which would end this present age. Those who were in Christ would be saved, those who were not would be destroyed (see the two passages in 1 Thess. just cited; further Phil. 3: 10 f. (resurrection) and 3: 19 (destruction)).

Yet Jesus' dreadful death, as a condemned criminal, was also central to Paul's message. When he wrote to the Galatians, he recalled that he had 'placarded' before their eyes Jesus Christ as crucified (Gal. 3: 1), and he reminded the Corinthians that he had known nothing among them 'except Jesus Christ and him crucified' (1 Cor. 2: 2).

Jesus' crucifixion, then, the beginning of the Christian proclamation, was not a defeat, but a step to ultimate redemption. It was for the believers' benefit, as is argued in a passage based on a pre-Pauline formula:

Since all have sinned and fall short of the glory of God, they are justified by his grace as a gift, through the redemption which is in Christ Jesus, whom God put forward as an expiation by his blood, to be received by faith. (Rom. 3: 23–5)

In these and many other passages we see the emphasis of the Christian message: (1) God had sent his Son; (2) he was crucified, but for the benefit of humanity; (3) he was raised from the dead and exalted to heaven; (4) he would soon return, and those who belonged to him would live with him forever. Paul's gospel, like that of others, also included (5) admonition to live by the highest ethical and moral standard: 'May your spirit and soul and body be kept sound and blameless at the coming of our Lord Jesus Christ' (1 Thess. 5: 23).

The sermons attributed to the apostles in Acts agree fairly closely with what we learn from the letters about Paul's basic missionary message. Acts contains several sermons by Peter, Jesus' chief disciple and later the chief apostle. This is the best short example:

Men of Israel, hear these words: Jesus of Nazareth, a man attested to you by God with mighty works and wonders and signs which God did through him in your midst, as you yourselves know—this Jesus, delivered up according to the definite plan and foreknowledge of God, you crucified and killed by the hands of lawless men. But God raised him up, having loosed the pangs of death ... This Jesus God raised up, and of that we all are witnesses. Being therefore exalted at the right hand of God, and having received from the Father the promise of the Holy Spirit, he has poured out this which you see and hear. (Acts 2: 22–4, 32–3)

'This which you see and hear' refers to the disciples' speaking in tongues, a charismatic gift which they attributed to the Spirit. In this sermon, besides the reference to the Spirit, we see another important point, one which is of the greatest relevance for understanding the development of the gospels. Jesus was 'attested to you by God with mighty works'. This is the seed which would grow, as time went on, into the great tree of the gospels: it became necessary to tell of Jesus' deeds.

Paul, however, has very little to say about the life of Jesus. He occasionally cites his words (as he seems to do in 1 Thess. 4: 15–18, speaking of 'the word of the Lord'). The only other teaching which he quotes is the prohibition of divorce (1 Cor. 7: 10–11; see also Matt. 5: 31–2; Luke 16: 18; Matt. 19: 3–9; Mark 10: 2–12). In addition to these teachings, he repeats Jesus' words at the last supper (1 Cor. 11: 23–5; see also Mark 14: 22–5 and parallels). Of his deeds Paul says nothing, at least not in the surviving correspondence. Paul's message focused on God's saving action in sending his Son and in raising him. This, Paul and the others held, assured believers that they would share his life.

The other difference between Paul's summaries of what he preached and Peter's sermons in Acts is that the former emphasize the nearness of the return of the Lord. As time passed, and the Lord did not return, this motif receded. The author of Acts probably revised Peter's sermons accordingly.

Modern people have a difficult time seeing how believable the basic message was to many ancients. If we now heard the proclamation of resurrection, the first questions would probably be, 'How do you know he was really dead?' and 'What was the resurrection like, what form did it take?' These questions did later come up, and Paul replied to the second in 1 Corinthians 15: 36–50. (His answer, which we shall consider in the next chapter, was that the resurrection was of a spiritual body, not a

23

physical body, not 'flesh and blood'.) The first question in the ancient world, where many believed that humans were basically immortal, seems to have been, 'How do we know that God raised *this* man to heaven and appointed him *Lord*?' Paul testified to his own vision of and commissioning by the risen Lord (1 Cor. 9: 1; 15: 8), and it is evident that many believed him and accepted Jesus as their saviour.

Powerful acts

Besides offering this simple message, Paul performed miracles which established his authority as a true prophet or spokesman of God. He wrote to the Thessalonians that 'our gospel came to you not only in word, but also in power and the Holy Spirit' (1 Thess. 1: 5). 'Power' is *dynamis*, 'mighty deed', often with the meaning 'miracle'. When the Corinthians, inspired by other apostles, doubted that Paul was a true apostle, or at least a good one, he reminded them that he had done the 'signs' (*semeia*) of a true apostle, including 'signs and wonders' (*terata*) and 'powerful acts' (*dynameis*) (2 Cor. 12: 12; cf. Rom. 15: 18 f.; 1 Cor. 2: 4). Some of his converts could also do *dynameis*, and they had charismatic gifts (*charismata*): Gal. 3: 5; 1 Cor. 1: 7; 7: 7; 12: 1, 4, 10 f., 28 f. These gifts included speaking in tongues, interpreting them, and healing (for example, 1 Cor. 12: 1, 10, 28), but for the most part 'powerful acts' are unspecified (for example, 1 Cor. 12: 28). Paul was prepared, however, to challenge his rebellious church in Corinth about their 'power' and to assert that he might come there and demonstrate his own:

Some are arrogant as though I were not coming to you. But I will come to you soon, if the Lord wills, and I will find out not the talk of these arrogant people but their power. For the kingdom of God does not consist in talk but in power. What do you wish? Shall I come to you with a rod or with love in a spirit of gentleness? (1 Cor. 4: 19–21)

We would like to know what these powers were. We know that Paul could speak in tongues 'more than you all' (1 Cor. 14: 18), and he saw visions (2 Cor. 12: 2–4, 7). Acts depicts him as healing and exorcizing (Acts 16: 16–18; 19: 11–12), and even as raising the dead (20: 7–12), but Paul himself says nothing of his own miracles. That he did things which were counted in the ancient world as miracles, however, need not be doubted.

Despite boasting of his 'power', when pressed for signs of his apostolic authority Paul appealed more to 'weakness' than to miracles, and more to the results of his missionary work than to his prowess. In the midst of assuring the Corinthians that he had performed the mighty deeds expected of an apostle, he also wrote, 'I will all the more gladly boast of my weaknesses, that the power of Christ may rest upon me' (2 Cor. 12: 9). We noted earlier that Paul was not especially impressive in person, yet he was an effective missionary. He saw in this the power of God working through his own weakness. The Lord said to him, 'my power is made perfect in weakness' (2 Cor. 12: 9), and the existence of Paul's churches showed that this was true (2 Cor. 3: 2–3).

4 The return of the Lord and the resurrection of the dead

Jesus' own expectation that the Kingdom of God was near had apparently led his followers to expect a divine intervention in history and the establishment of God's rule in the world, not just in the hearts and minds of a few. His execution temporarily undermined the disciples' expectation, but the resurrection convinced them that their former master was now their Lord and that he would return to establish his kingdom.

We saw above that the third central part of the early Christian proclamation was precisely this: the Lord would soon return to save his followers and establish his reign. 1 Thessalonians makes it clear that Paul taught his converts that the Lord would return so soon that they would live to see the day, but we also see that this expectation was challenged by events.

We owe it to difficulties in Paul's churches that he became a 'theologian', one who developed a rationale and an explanation for his basic religious beliefs. Of the five fundamental convictions listed above (p. 22), all but the first two (God sent Christ to save the world, and he was crucified) became the subject of debate or even hostile controversy among Christians. The implication of the resurrection was disputed in Corinth; the delay of the Lord's return resulted in questions in Thessalonica; the meaning of 'those who have faith' led to an extremely fierce debate, which is seen in Galatians directly and in Romans slightly more distantly; Christians even disagreed about ethical behaviour. We shall examine these problem areas in this and the succeeding chapters.

The return of the Lord and the fate of Christians, living and dead

The issue which we encounter first in Paul's correspondence (reading it chronologically) is the return of the Lord, which is one of the chief topics of 1 Thessalonians. This will lead us into a discussion of the nature of the resurrection.

The problem in Thessalonica was that some members had died, and the survivors worried about their fate. This indicates the thrust of Paul's original message: not that believers would be resurrected, but rather that they would live to be saved when the Lord returned. Death was not expected. Paul wrote to re-assure the survivors that the dead would not miss the return of the Lord. This assurance, he hoped, would prevent the Thessalonian Christians from grieving 'as others do who have no hope' (1 Thess. 4: 13). The ground for confidence was that 'Jesus died and rose again', and thus those who belonged to him, even if they died, would be given life with him (4: 14).

Paul then gives what he calls 'a word of the Lord'. Scholars debate the meaning of the term, most taking the view that the saying is a revelation made to a Christian prophet rather than a teaching of the historical Jesus. I incline the other way, but for the present this issue need not be debated. In either case, Paul designates what follows as not merely his own view: it is from 'the Lord'. Sayings which are very similar to Paul's 'word of the Lord' are attributed to Jesus in the gospels. If we compare these with Paul's, and further note the particular circumstances to which Paul needed to apply the saying, we can identify his own modifications. That is, despite his intention to quote an earlier tradition, he altered it to fit the present circumstances. In particular, he applied a saying which did not originally mention the dead to the concern of the Thessalonians about what would happen to Christians who died before the return of the Lord. In the quotation which follows Paul's probable modifications are in italic type:

For this we declare to you by the word of the Lord, that we who are alive, who are left until the coming of the Lord, *shall not precede those who have fallen asleep. For the Lord himself* will descend from heaven with a cry of command, with the archangel's call, and with the sound of the trumpet of God. *And the dead in Christ will rise first*; then we who are alive, who are left, *shall be caught up together with them in the clouds to meet the Lord in the air*; and so we shall always be with the Lord. (1 Thess. 4: 15–18)

Sayings attributed to Jesus in the gospels predict that, in the hearers' lifetime, the Son of man will descend with angels and the sound of a trumpet (Matt. 16: 27–8; 24: 30–1). Thus this expectation arose early (as its use in 1 Thessalonians shows), and many Christians thought that it stemmed from Jesus. Paul's statement differs from the passages in the gospels in these ways: (1) Paul writes in the first person, 'we', whereas the sayings in the gospels refer to 'you'. This is merely an editorial change. (2) He speaks of 'the Lord's' return rather than of the appearance of the Son of man. This shows the Christian assumption that the Son of man referred to by Jesus was identical with himself. (3) Paul takes account of those who have already died, and says that they will precede the living. This is his principal modification to meet the problems in Thessalonica. (4) The statement that believers will go up to meet the Lord 'in the clouds . . . in the air' has no parallel in the gospels.

The expectation that 'we' would still be alive may have been common in Christian circles, while the sequence of 'first the dead then the living' was Paul's own, devised for the situation which he faced. Thus whatever the precise history of this tradition, the explicit provision for the dead seems to be Paul's, and it was made to meet the problem in Thessalonica. A concrete difficulty produced a change in the tradition.

The nature of the resurrection

The fourth distinctive point, 'in the air', leads us into an exploration of what Paul expected. It seems that he thought neither that Christians who were still alive when the Lord returned would fly up to heaven in their natural bodies, nor that their inner souls would leave their bodies behind. This becomes clear in the Corinthian correspondence. The Corinthian converts, or at least some of them, denied the future resurrection (see 1 Cor. 15: 13 f.). Apparently they thought that the spiritual gifts which they had already received *constituted* the new life: already they were 'kings' (1 Cor. 4: 8). Paul emphasized that what was most important lay ahead. As in 1 Thessalonians, he equated the future state of the living with that of the dead in Christ: they will all be *transformed*.

> Lo! I tell you a mystery. We shall not all sleep, but we shall all be changed, in a moment, in the twinkling of an eye, at the last trumpet. For the trumpet will sound, and the dead will be raised imperishable, and we shall be changed. (1 Cor. 15: 51–2)

The change would make them like the risen Lord. 'Just as we have borne the image of the man of dust [Adam], we shall also bear the image of the man of heaven [Christ]' (1 Cor. 15: 49). Just what would this be like? Paul understandably had difficulty in saying precisely what the transformed body would be. He was convinced that he had seen the risen Lord (1 Cor. 9: 1), and thus it follows that the 'man of heaven' was both visible and identifiable. On the other hand, there had been (and would be) a real transformation. 'Flesh and blood cannot inherit the kingdom of heaven' (1 Cor. 15: 50). The chief characteristic of bodies of flesh and blood is that they are perishable, and the perishable cannot inherit what is imperishable (15: 42, 50).

Paul, that is, thought of the resurrected Jesus neither as a corpse which had regained the ability to breathe and walk nor as a ghost. He regarded Jesus as 'first fruits' of the resurrection (1 Cor. 15: 20) and thought that all Christians would become like him. He denied that the resurrected body would be the 'natural' body, but maintained that it would be a 'spiritual' body (1 Cor. 15: 44–6). 'Not a natural body' excludes a walking corpse, while 'spiritual body' excludes a ghost (which would be called in Greek simply a 'spirit', *pneuma*). Positively, there would be continuity between the ordinary and the resurrected person, as there was in the case of Jesus. To express this, Paul used the simile of seed, which, when planted, is in one form, but, when grown, in another (1 Cor. 15: 36–8).

The degree to which he thought of 'transformation', rather than either disembodiment or resuscitation, can be seen in his discussion of 'putting on' immortality. Thinking of those who would still be alive when the Lord returned, he wrote that the 'perishable nature must put on the imperishable, and this

mortal nature must put on immortality'. This would fulfil the
Scripture, 'Death is swallowed up in victory' (1 Cor. 15: 53 f.).
He used the same imagery in 2 Corinthians 5. The living are in
an 'earthly tent', and they wish not to be 'unclothed', 'but that we
would be further clothed, so that what is mortal may be swallowed up by life' (2 Cor. 5: 4). The metaphor changes from
'tent' to 'clothing', but the meaning is nevertheless clear. Immortality is 'put on' and replaces mortality. Paul was not thinking of an interior soul which escapes its mortal shell and floats
free, nor of new life being breathed into the same body, but
again of transformation, achieved by covering mortality with
immortality, which then 'swallows' it.

Conceivably, had Paul known about atoms and molecules, he
would have put all this in different terms. What he is affirming
and denying is clear: resurrection means transformed body, not
walking corpse or disembodied spirit. We can hardly criticize
him for not being able to define 'spiritual body' more clearly.
His information on the topic was almost certainly derived entirely from his experience of encountering the risen Lord—an
experience which he does not describe in his letters. That experience led him to the statements we have seen, which stop a
good deal short of being a full definition. We cannot describe
that experience on his behalf and then improve on his definition
of the resurrected body, and we must be content to know only
what he thought.

The end of the world

Did Paul think that the return of the Lord, the transformation
of the living and the raising of the dead, meant 'the end of the
world'? It is possible to construe 1 Thessalonians 4: 13–18 in that
way: the transformed believers meet the Lord in the air and stay
there, and the kingdom is in heaven. It is more likely, though, that
Paul thought that they would ascend to meet the Lord and then
return to earth with him. According to Philippians 3: 20 f. the
Christians' 'commonwealth' is in heaven, and they expect their
saviour to come from there. He is probably coming for a purpose: to establish his reign on earth. Similarly in 2 Corinthians

5: 1 f., Paul speaks of 'putting on' the building that comes from heaven; that is, it will come down and engulf what is mortal ('from heaven' is not clear in most translations). Finally, we note that Paul expected the entire physical universe to be transformed. 'Creation itself will be set free from its bondage to decay' (Rom. 8: 21). It is very likely, then, that Paul accepted the common Christian view that Jesus would establish his reign on earth, but on a transformed earth, one no longer subject to decay.

On the other hand, 1 Corinthians 15: 24 f. points towards a final dissolution of the world: after Christ has reigned for a while, and destroyed all enemies, he will hand the kingdom over to God. The Son himself will be subjected to God, that 'God may be all in all' (so, correctly, the New English Bible (NEB), Jerusalem Bible (JB), and New International Version (NIV); the RSV misleadingly has 'may be everything to every one').

Going to be with the Lord immediately after death

Another difficulty led to a different formulation of the future expectation. The difficulty was Paul's own imprisonment at the time he wrote Philippians. We do not know just when or where that was, and so we cannot say that a chronological development had taken place, but the imprisonment did make Paul consider the possibility of his own death before the return of the Lord. In some ways he hoped for it:

Even if I am to be poured as a libation upon the sacrificial offering of your faith, I am glad and rejoice with you all. (Phil. 2: 17)

For to me to live is Christ, and to die is gain. If it is to be life in the flesh, that means fruitful labour for me. Yet which I shall choose I cannot tell. I am hard pressed between the two. My desire is to depart and be with Christ, for that is far better. But to remain in the flesh is more necessary on your account. Convinced of this, I know that I shall remain. (Phil. 1: 21–5)

Here we see that Paul thought that if he died he would 'depart' and 'be with Christ'. Conceptually, this is different from the expectation of the transformation or resurrection of all

31

believers at the coming of the Lord. We see here the Greek idea of the immortality of the soul, which is individualistic rather than communal. It envisages the ascent of each person's soul at death, rather than the transformation of the entire group of believers, whether living or dead, at Christ's return. Without posing these two conceptions to himself as alternatives, Paul simply accepted them both. If he died, he would immediately be with Christ; at the end the Lord would return and bring his own, in a transformed state, to be with him.

The present beginning of the transformation

In 2 Corinthians 3: 12–5: 10 we see further efforts to formulate what the final state of the believers would be. They will be transformed, but Paul considers that the transformation is already under way: 'we all . . . reflecting the glory of the Lord, are being changed into his likeness from one degree of glory to another' (2 Cor. 3: 18); 'though our outer nature is wasting away, our inner nature is being renewed every day' (4: 18). On the one hand, the transformation from the old to the 'new creation' is already in progress; on the other, the process is not visible but internal.

Paul returns to the more purely Greek notion of the soul in the body, from which it may escape: 'while we are at home in the body we are away from the Lord . . . we would rather be away from the body and at home with the Lord' (2 Cor. 5: 6–8).

Some have sought a chronological development from the 'Jewish' idea of the resurrection of everyone at the same time to the 'Greek' idea of the immortality of individual souls. This, however, is not the explanation. In 2 Corinthians 3–5 we find successively 'inner renewal' (3: 18), the promise of resurrection (4: 14) and the idea that the individual, to be 'at home with the Lord', must be 'away from the body' (5: 6–8). What appear to be conceptually different ideas lie side by side.

The neat distinction between 'Greek' and 'Jewish' categories is probably a bit misleading. Not only were they not posed as alternatives by Paul, it is quite possible that some Diaspora synagogues had long since combined immortality and resurrection. In later Jewish and Christian literature they would be explicitly harmonized: at death the soul ascends to heaven, to await the resurrection; at the resurrection soul and body are reunited.

The expectation of the end of the present world order—one of Paul's central convictions—appears too in what may be his last surviving letter, Romans ('may be' because Philippians and Philemon, the prison epistles, cannot be dated):

Besides this you know what hour it is, how it is full time now for you to wake from sleep. For salvation is nearer to us now than when we first believed; the night is far gone, the day is at hand. (Rom. 13: 11–12)

Thus Paul, as long as we can follow his thought, continued to expect the arrival of the Lord. He had to alter aspects of this hope for certain situations—the crisis over the dead in Thessalonica and the possibility of his own death—and he also made use of the idea of individual immortality. But to the end his basic conviction remained.

5 Theological presuppositions: monotheism and providence

Before we can understand the major disputes in which Paul engaged, and his responses to them, we need to explain presuppositions which he brought to the debate, presuppositions which his Jewish contemporaries, both friend and foe, generally shared. Paul inherited from Judaism two principal theological views: there is one God; God controls the world. These two views might seem to turn history into a puppet show, but they were not held simplistically. Most Jews reckoned with other powers in the world besides God, and they thought that humans could exercise freedom of choice. God's control was usually seen as being exercised on a very large scale: ultimately the world would turn out as he intended. In general Jews did not deny that God could play a hand in everyday affairs, but they did not necessarily attribute every minor event to his will.

All of these points can be seen in Paul's letters: he believed in one God; he thought that there were other powers in the universe besides God; he thought that God was exercising a grand plan in history; and he thought that individuals could decide to be with him or against him.

The one God and enemy powers

In 1 Corinthians 8 Paul considers whether Christians should eat food that has been offered to an idol. Some of the Corinthian Christians wished to do so, arguing that the idols were not real. They accepted monotheism more radically than did Paul. He replied that although idols do not really exist and although there is only one God, nevertheless there are many so-called gods and lords. The Corinthians should not eat food offered to them because they might be misunderstood as believing in idols. Thus far it might seem that Paul accepts radical monotheism, but in chapter 10 he returns to the topic: 'What do I imply then? That food offered to idols is anything, or that an idol is anything? No, I imply that what pagans sacrifice they offer to demons and not to God' (1 Cor. 10: 19f.).

So: there are no other gods, but there are demons. The 'so-called gods and lords' of 1 Corinthians 8: 4–6 are not really Gods and Lords, but they are something. Paul speaks of them in other ways: 'beings that by nature are no gods' (as the RSV nicely translates a difficult phrase, Gal. 4: 8); Satan, who disguises himself as the 'angel of light' (2 Cor. 11: 14); 'another god', who governs 'this age' (2 Cor. 4: 4); 'rulers of this age' (1 Cor. 2: 6); 'principalities' and 'powers' (Rom. 8: 38), or 'principalities, authorities and powers' (1 Cor. 15: 24). There were knees to be bent not only on the earth, but also above and below it (Phil. 2: 10). In the end, Christ will triumph (Rom. 8: 38f.; 1 Cor. 15: 24–6; Phil. 2: 9–11), but meanwhile these beings can create a good deal of trouble.

We should pay special attention to the degree to which Sin is treated by Paul as an enemy power. This is most clearly the case when the noun *hamartia*, sin, is the subject of a verb other than 'to be', as it is in Romans 5–7. According to Romans 5: 12 Sin 'entered the world'; thereafter one reads that 'Sin reigned in death' (5: 21); that Sin may 'reign' in one's body (6: 12) or 'have dominion' over one (6: 14); that Sin found opportunity in the commandment and 'wrought in me all kinds of covetousness' (7: 8); that it 'revived' (7: 9); that it found 'opportunity in the commandment, deceived me and by it killed me' (7: 11); and that it 'worked death in me through what is good' (7: 13). Sin as power may be served (6: 16–18), and thus it enslaves (6: 20). Put another way, Sin is a 'law' which lurks in one's members and prevents the fulfilling of the law of God (7: 17–23). The only escape is to leave 'the Flesh' (8: 8), the domain of Sin, by sharing Christ's death. Christians have died with Christ and thus to Sin (6: 2–11), and they have thereby escaped not only Sin but also the law (which condemns) and the 'Flesh', the state of enmity towards God (7: 4–6).

We shall return to Sin in Romans 6–7 just below, but here a few words are required in explanation of the term 'the flesh'. Paul sometimes uses it to mean 'the physical body', but in this section of Romans it often refers to the state of humanity when it opposes God. Thus, strikingly, Romans 7: 5 f.: 'while we were living in the Flesh ... But now we are discharged from the law ... so that we serve not under the old written code but in the new life of the Spirit.' The 'we' refers to Paul and other Christians. They are no longer 'in the Flesh', though they are still in their skins with their body tissue intact. As Paul puts it in Romans 8: 9, 'You are not in the Flesh, you are in the Spirit', and the contrast of Flesh and Spirit continues (8: 9–13). My guess is that we see here the explanation of why Paul uses 'Flesh' to mean 'humanity in the state of opposition to God': it is simply the word which is opposite 'Spirit', which in turn denotes the divine power. This is, at any rate, the best way to decide when to capitalize Flesh, so that it points not to humanity as physical, but to humanity under an enemy power. It is the latter when there is a clear contrast between it and the Spirit of God. Then flesh becomes Flesh.

In this section of Romans Paul treats Sin as a power which is not only alien to God but almost as powerful; in fact, it often wins the struggle. It is important to note that Paul does not offer an anthropological, theological or cosmological explanation of this conception of Sin. In the Jewish view, God had created the world and declared it good, a teaching which is not easily reconcilable with the view that Sin is a power strong enough to wrest the law from God's control or to render humans powerless to do what is good (Rom. 7: 11, 19).

There are two principal passages which lead up to, but do not account for, the view that all humanity, apart from Christ, is under the power of Sin. In Romans 1–2 both Gentiles and Jews are accused of gross transgression (homosexuality and 'all manner of wickedness' on the part of Gentiles, robbing temples and committing adultery on the part of Jews), and Paul draws the conclusion that all people, 'both Jews and Greeks, are under sin' (Rom. 3: 9). The RSV here translates 'under sin' as 'under the *power* of sin' and this interpretation seems to correspond to Paul's meaning. The accusation is not just that people transgress, but that all are governed by Sin. The charges of heinous immorality, however, do not actually account for Paul's conclusion that *everyone* is under the power of Sin. This is so partly because his accusations are exaggerated. Both the Gentile and the Jewish worlds contained 'saints', people whose lives were largely beyond reproach. It is unlikely that Paul's view of universal heinous transgression rested on empirical observation. Further, in the midst of his catalogue of charges Paul admits that some Gentiles, though without the law, nevertheless 'do by nature what the law requires', and these will be justified by their works in the judgement (Rom. 2: 13–14). The conclusion in 3:9 does not correspond to what leads up to it in any respect: the charges in chapters 1–2 overstate the case and the conclusion is contradicted by 2: 13–14. What this means is that Paul's conclusion, that all are under Sin, was not derived from the line of observation and reasoning which he presents in the previous two chapters.

The same is true of Romans 5, where Paul also argues for the universality of sin. Adam, he states, sinned, and this introduced sin and its consequence, death, into the world; 'and so death spread to all people because all sinned' (Rom. 5: 12). This is followed by the statements that 'sin is not counted where there is no law' and that 'death reigned from Adam to Moses, *even over* those whose sins were not like the transgression of Adam' (5: 13–14). In order to make the grip of sin universal, Paul wished to make Adam instrumental. Yet he had two problems: transgressions of the law which preceded the giving of it should not count; not everyone sinned, as did Adam, by rebelling against God's commandment. Despite these problems he asserted the consequence: 'by one man's disobedience many were made sinners' (5: 19). His anthropology (unlike Augustine's) did not include the conception of inherited sin, and thus he had no logical way of 'proving' universal condemnation by appeal to Adam. He simply asserted it—while himself citing points which count against it.

What we see in both cases is a conclusion that is independent of the arguments which precede it. Adam's sin does not, in Paul's own statement of it, prove that all humanity is sinful and stands condemned. The heinous sins of some Greeks and Jews do not, even in Paul's own presentation of them, lead to the view that all humans are enslaved by Sin. This means that he held the conclusion as a fixed view and tried to bring forward arguments in favour of it, though without logical success. The conclusion, in other words, is not only independent of but is also more important than the arguments.

If the considerations put forward in Romans 1–2 and 5 do not explain the origin of Paul's conception of Sin, can we say where it came from? There are two principal possibilities. One is that Paul did not come to Christianity with a pre-formed conception of humanity's sinful plight, but rather deduced the plight from the solution. Once he accepted it as revelation that God intended to save the entire world by sending his Son, he naturally had to think that the entire world needed saving, and thus that it was wholly bound over to Sin. His soteriology is more consistent and straightforward than are his conceptions of the human plight. It seems that his fixed view of salvation forced him to go in search of arguments in favour of universal sin. This explains why Romans 1–2 and 5 are so weak as reasoned arguments but lead to such a definite conclusion. The conclusion that all need to be saved through Christ, since Paul received it as revelation, could not be questioned; the arguments in favour of universal bondage to Sin, then, are efforts at rationalization.

That is one explanation. The second is that Paul had imbibed aspects of a dualistic world view, according to which the created order is at least partly under the control of the god of darkness. Iranian (Zoroastrian) dualism had penetrated the Mediterranean, and it can be seen in the Dead Sea Scrolls, for example, when they distinguish between the angel of darkness and the angel of light, the children of darkness and the children of light (for example, *Community Rule* 3: 17–4: 1). There are echoes of this terminology in Paul. In 2 Corinthians 11: 14, where Satan is said to disguise himself as the 'angel of light', Satan is, in effect, the 'angel of darkness'.

It is probable that Paul had been influenced by dualism, especially since he considered the entire created order to be in need of redemption (Rom. 8: 19–23), though it could not have been guilty of transgression. But here we see that despite some influence of dualism, Paul was not a dualist. He proposed that it was God himself who had subjected the creation to 'futility', and that he had done so 'in hope', planning its redemption. Formally, there is no admission in Romans 8 of a second power, much less a second god. Yet Paul did believe in evil spiritual forces which he called by various names, as we noted above. These non-gods could blind (2 Cor. 4: 4) and enslave (Gal. 4: 8), as could Sin (Rom. 6: 6).

If there is some truth in the suggestion that Paul was influenced by dualistic thought, there is more in the view that his discussions of sin are the reflex of his soteriology. We see the force of the latter most fully when we consider his view of God's work in history, which we may call 'providence', and then ask about the relationship between providence and sin.

Providence

Jews commonly held that God controls history, both its main movements and selected individual moments. It will be useful briefly to illustrate the idea as it occurs in Josephus, the Jewish priest who became Judaism's historian. He was born in 37 CE, and thus was Paul's younger contemporary. We shall fix especially on the hardest part of Josephus's own theology, the view that God himself intended Rome to be the dominant world power, and in particular decided that the great Jewish revolt (66–73/4) should fail. This was, to be sure, punishment for transgression. As the war with Rome approached, assassins had shed blood in the sanctuary, and it needed to be purged with fire (*Jewish War*, 4: 201; 5: 19); the people had broken the law (for example, by fighting on the Sabbath: ibid., 2: 517 f.), and they deserved punishment. God chose as his instruments Vespasian and Titus, the Roman father and son who reconquered Jewish Palestine.

Josephus's theory that God chose Vespasian and Titus to accomplish the punishment of Israel allows us to illustrate the fact that relatively minor moments could be explained as being determined by God. According to one story, Titus was reconnoitring, without his armour, when he was cut off from his

39

scouting party by an ambush. The hail of arrows missed him, and he escaped unharmed. This showed, according to Josephus, that 'the hazards of war and the perils of princes are under God's care' (*Jewish War*, 5: 60). He notes that 'it is impossible for people to escape their fate', but also that 'the Jews' had interpreted this and other portents in a different way. He piously observes that God cares for people, 'and by all kinds of premonitory signs shows his people the way of salvation, while they owe their destruction to folly and calamities of their own choosing' (ibid., 6: 310–15).

Josephus's theologizing was very much after the fact. He knew the outcome: Vespasian, who started the campaign against the rebellious Jews, was proclaimed emperor; his son Titus, who completed it, succeeded him; Jerusalem was destroyed, while Rome flourished. Looking backwards, through the lens of that last great fact, Josephus saw the conclusion as planned by God, and he then construed events leading up to the destruction as also planned by God. He saw God as warning the Jews along the way that this would happen. They exercised free will, they refused to understand the oracles and portents correctly, they clung to their own path and ignored God's, and so they correctly met their doom. God determined the outcome; they deserved it.

This is a powerful theology, because it explains everything. It is, however, subject to ridicule. It was easy for Josephus in retrospect to say that what actually happened was planned, since in retrospect God's plan can be made to coincide perfectly with what actually happened.

We should not, however, rush into ridicule. The idea of God's providence, which is trivialized when it is applied to the control of the flight of arrows, includes the idea that God wills what is good for the entire universe. This idea, in turn, is tied to the doctrine of creation. God created the universe, he cares for it, he governs it, and his will towards it is beneficent. Few will find this ridiculous, many have found and do find it comforting. Any theology which can see the entire created order in such a positive light is a noble one. The doctrine of creation, allied with the general idea of God's providence, is one of Judaism's noblest

gifts to humanity. Josephus may have trivialized it, but everything can be trivialized. Great principles have the power to
survive and be rekindled, and so it is with Judaism's great
doctrine.

Paul shared all these points. He thought 'backwards' from the
revealed solution—that God sent Christ to save the world—to
the plight from which he saved it—that all things were 'under
Sin'. He thought that God controlled the world and history as a
whole; he saw him especially at work in some particular events.
Looking back through the lens of the appearance of Christ to
him, Paul saw everything as leading up to that event, and the
rest of history as being determined by it. The revelation drove
Paul to preach to the Gentiles, and so he thought that God had
always planned to save the Gentiles by faith in his Son. Looking
back, Paul saw the election of Abraham himself as pointing
towards the inclusion of the Gentiles (see Chapter 6 below). But
since God, in Paul's new insight, had sent Christ to save the
world, both everybody and everything, it was necessary to conclude that he had not previously provided for its salvation. Thus
the lead-up to universal salvation was negative: the world previously must have been condemned, and whatever preceded
Christ must have served to put it in that condition.

This means that God himself had intended that the world was
enslaved to Sin, so that he could save it. This idea may seem
impious, but Paul did not hesitate to affirm it. The law itself, he
proposed, was given by God to condemn, so that all could be
saved by God's mercy as manifested in Christ (Gal. 3: 22).
Finally, however, God's beneficent purpose towards all would
be accomplished. Paul did not know precisely how: it was a
mystery, but somehow all Israel would be saved (Rom. 11:
25–6). And not only Israel: 'For God has consigned all people
to disobedience, that he may have mercy upon all' (Rom. 11:
32). Condemnation had included the entire created order (he
condemned *ta panta*, all things, Gal. 3: 22), but so would salvation: the whole creation 'has been groaning in travail together
until now' (Rom. 8: 22). The passages in which Paul attributes
to God the intention to condemn will occupy us more fully in
Chapter 9, and we shall consider whether or not Paul really

41

believed in universal salvation in Chapter 11. Just now we note that these two ideas arise from the fundamental theology of God's providence.

We would not want to say that Paul trivialized the doctrine of providence. He focused salvation on faith in Christ, which some will find to be the wrong focus, or too narrow a focus, but the grandeur of the theology of creation and providence is fully present, and its universal scope is preserved in Paul's vision of the impending future.

In the passages which state that God intended to condemn the world so that he could later save it, we see the combination of Paul's twin convictions: the one God is the God of Hebrew Scripture, the one who created the world, who called Abraham and who gave the law; and the same God always intended to save the world by faith in Christ. Thinking backwards from the second point, he had to conclude that the prior divine acts—creation, election and the law—did not save. In his black-and-white world, if they did not save they did not even help; election and the law were not stepping-stones to salvation in Christ. Yet God gave the law. What is its result? Not salvation, therefore damnation. This meant that God intended the result, he 'consigned all to disobedience'. One might say that humanity was consigned to iniquity as the result of prior sin, which stirred God to wrath (Rom. 1: 18, 24). But in Romans 1 this is used only to account for Gentile corruption, and it is the result of idolatry. The giving of the law cannot be attributed to God's wrath in the same way. Paul's monotheism, which included the view that God controlled *everything* that happened, was braver than that. God intended human sinfulness, just as he intended the subjection of the non-human world to 'futility' and 'travail', but throughout he intended good (Rom. 8: 28): the salvation of the entire cosmos.

No form of ancient Judaism directly known to us (that is, possibly excluding Sadduceeism) considered 'predestination' and 'free will' to be incompatible. In Qumran the members of the community were called both 'the elect' and 'the volunteers'; they were gravely warned not to disobey, but wickedness was also attributed to the 'angel' who governed their 'lot'. Paul puts the two side by side as well. Most Jews, he wrote, did not accept Jesus because God 'hardened' them; on the other hand, they did not 'heed' (Rom. 10: 7, 16). When Paul, like many other Jewish thinkers, applied predestination and free will to the problem of sin, the result was both that God intended it and that humans were nevertheless guilty. No ancient Jew, including Paul, worked out a consistent explanation of how human decision to sin relates to God's determination of all that happens. Paul at least dealt seriously with the problem, as Romans 9 shows. Dualism provides an alternative: there are two powers which have different intentions, and humans are pulled first one way then the other. In Paul we get all three. Sin is avoidable transgression, and it is therefore punishable; Sin is a power external to humanity which enslaves the entire creation; sin was intended by God in order to lead up negatively to salvation through his grace in Christ.

In the discussion of the law in Chapter 9 we shall see that, despite his bravery, Paul was uncomfortable holding that God had given the law in order to condemn, and that he temporarily retracted this view in Romans 7, especially in verse 10. It was in trying to avoid laying the intention to condemn at God's door that Paul shifted to a modified dualism. Sin is an external power which can manipulate the law (7: 8), or it is a power within the flesh (7: 18, 23) in defiance of the goodness of creation. The presence of dualistic influence in Romans 6–7 cannot be denied, and it is confirmed by the passages about inimical non-gods. Yet in the discussion of sin there is a more powerful theology at work which runs throughout his thought: God created the world and controls history; he will save the world through Christ; everything else, *even sin itself*, follows from his will but is subjected to it and used for his purpose.

6 Righteousness by faith and being in Christ: Galatians

The Lord, Christians agreed, would return and save those who belonged to him. This posed a very obvious problem: who belonged to him? Obviously those who accepted him as Lord. But 'Lord' did not tell the whole story. He was also the expected 'anointed one' who would redeem Israel ('anointed' in Hebrew produces the word 'Messiah', while the Greek translation results in the word 'Christ'). If he was the Messiah or Christ of Israel, would he, at his return, save only those who both accepted him *and* were Jews in good standing? This question brings us to a central and difficult topic in Galatians and Romans, Paul's so-called 'doctrine' of 'righteousness by faith'. The inverted commas indicate that neither term is entirely appropriate.

Paul's thought contains one overarching difficulty, and he himself was aware of it: how does God's recent revelation in Christ relate to his former revelations to Israel? Apart from this central difficulty, Paul's views about the topics that fall under the present heading are not hard to discover and understand— that is, understand as well as modern people can, granted that we do not entirely share his world-view. Yet what he wrote about faith, righteousness, participation in Christ and the Jewish law has led to endless debate and puzzlement. There are three problems, one of which plagues only English-speakers and one of which plagues only people in modern times, but they all have to be sorted out: English is deficient in its ability to translate the key terms, and English translations are consequently confusing; Paul himself sometimes used the language of 'righteousness' in a peculiar way; Martin Luther, whose influence on subsequent interpreters has been enormous, made Paul's statements central to his own quite different theology.

Preliminary difficulties

We begin with the problem of English translations. Modern English has two parents, Norman French and Anglo-Saxon. In most cases this gives the English-speaker a richness of vocabulary which few other languages equal. We distinguish the Anglo-Saxon 'swine' (tended by Anglo-Saxon peasants in the field) from the French 'pork' (eaten by the conquering Normans at table). Anglo-Saxon was a Germanic language, and to this day Germans eat *Schweinfleisch*, 'swine flesh', which strikes the English-speaker as crude and unpalatable. In the dual vocabulary which its two parents afford English, words derived from Anglo-Saxon often have a common or earthy meaning (like 'swine'), while those derived from French are more polite or sophisticated. This reflects the fact that the Normans won the battle of Hastings and became the English nobility. The dual parentage usually allows us to make fine distinctions and nuances.

In the case of key words in Paul's vocabulary, however, we have a difficulty, since some forms drove others out, rather than remaining as duplicates. The best translation of Paul's word *dikaiosynē* is the Anglo-Saxon 'righteousness', not the French 'justification', since 'justification' often carries the nuance of defensiveness or of a legal excuse, and we shall see that this was not Paul's meaning. Paul's cognate verb, *dikaioun*, however, no longer has an Anglo-Saxon equivalent. The verb *rihtwísian* was lost long ago, and we have only the French 'justify'.[†]

Similary 'faith' best translates Paul's *pistis*, since 'belief' often connotes 'opinion', which is far from what Paul meant. But English has no verb which corresponds to 'faith', and so for Paul's verb *pisteuein* English translators have to use 'believe'. In this case the Anglo-Saxon verb has driven out the French. A table will make the problem clear.

[†] The Anglo-Saxon forms were these: rihtwís[e], n.: 'righteousness' or 'rightness'; rihtwís, adj.: 'righteous'; rihtwísian, v.: 'rightwise'. It is this last form which has been lost. Anglo-Saxon had the further adjective and noun: rihtwíslíc, 'righteous'; rihtwísness, 'righteousness'.

Terminology for righteousness and faith

	Greek	Anglo-Saxon	French
Noun	*dikaiosynē*	righteousness	justification
Adj.	*dikaios*	righteous	just
Verb	*dikaioun*		to justify
Noun	*pistis*	belief	faith
Adj.	*pistos*	believing	faithful
Verb	*pisteuein*	to believe	

We would like to be able to use the words derived from Anglo-Saxon to translate all the 'righteousness' terminology and the words derived from French to translate all the 'faith' terminology, but in each case there is no cognate verb in English. The resulting problems of translation can readily be exemplified. In Gal. 3: 6–7 Paul, quoting Gen. 15: 6, wrote this (according to the RSV):

Thus Abraham '*believed* God, and it was reckoned to him as *righteousness*'. So you see that it is people of *faith* who are the sons of Abraham. And the scripture, foreseeing that God would *justify* the Gentiles by *faith*, preached the gospel beforehand to Abraham.

Paul did not actually change terms from 'believe' to 'faith' or from 'righteousness' to 'justify'. With regard to the first set, he used the verb *pisteuein* ('believe') when quoting Genesis to prove that people of *pistis* ('faith') are 'justified'. Similarly he wrote first the noun *dikaiosynē* and then the verb *dikaioun*, and the quoted passage, which mentions 'righteousness', serves to prove the conclusion that God 'justifies', except that in English the connection is lost. To see the way Paul actually argued—in this case, from terms in the Greek version of the Old Testament—we must in each case translate the verb and the noun by using the same English root, and the best way to proceed is to keep the better nouns, 'righteousness' and 'faith', and to use verbs which correspond to them. For the verb which goes with 'faith', I shall use 'to have faith in', but in the case of a verb which agrees with 'righteousness' a more radical solution is required, and I shall restore an old verb in modern dress: 'to righteous'. This is less drastic and more justifiable (pun intended) than using 'to author' to mean 'to write' or 'to compose'. Though we do not yet know what Paul meant by the verb, we at least have a term that allows us to follow the argument in English. The resulting translation of Galatians 3: 6–7 is this:

Thus Abraham '*had faith in* God, and it was reckoned to him as *righteousness*'. So you see that it is men of *faith* who are the sons of Abraham. And the scripture, foreseeing that God would *righteous* the Gentiles by *faith* . . .

Now the words of Genesis 15: 6, 'have faith in' and 'righteousness', are correctly correlated with Paul's conclusion: God righteouses Gentiles by faith. The same technique clarifies Galatians 2: 16. Instead of '[Since we] know that a man is not justified by works of the law but through faith in Jesus Christ, even we have believed . . . in order to be justified by faith', we now read, '[Since we] know that a person is not righteoused by works of the law but through faith in Jesus Christ, even we have had faith . . . in order to be righteoused by faith.'

Even if we were not plagued by these curious and unusual defects of English, Paul would still be hard to understand. The Greek verb *dikaioun*, 'to righteous', ordinarily means 'to regard someone who is right as being in the right'—that is, to consider or declare the guiltless to be innocent. This, the 'judicial' meaning of the word ('judicial' because it recalls the language of the lawcourt) is the principal and normal meaning of the terms for 'righteousness' both in Greek and English (except that for legal terminology English ordinarily uses 'just' and its cognates, such as 'justice'). The *dikai-* word group not infrequently has the expected judicial meaning in Paul's letters. Thus, for example, Romans 5: 18: 'Then as one man's trespass led to condemnation for all men, so one man's act of righteousness (*dikaiōma*) leads to rightness (*dikaiōsis*) and life for all men.' Here *dikaiōsis* is often and accurately translated 'acquittal': it is the reverse of condemnation, and the entire sentence is couched in terms of legal guilt or innocence.

Paul also, however, presses the meaning of the verb *dikaioun*, 'to righteous', beyond this, its normal frame of reference.

47

We know that our old self was crucified with him so that the sinful body might be destroyed, and we might no longer be *enslaved* to sin. For he who has died is *righteoused* from sin. (Rom. 6: 6–7)

The opposite of 'enslaved' is not to be declared innocent or upright, and a few verses later Paul finds a more appropriate word:

you are slaves of the one whom you obey ... But thanks be to God, that you who were once *slaves* of sin have become obedient ... and, *having been set free* from sin ... (Rom. 6: 16–18)

Here the opposite of being enslaved is correctly called 'being set free', and substantively this must also be the meaning of 6: 7—where, however, Paul used the word 'righteoused'.

The passive verb 'to be righteoused' in Paul's letters almost always means to be *changed*, to be *transferred* from one realm to another: from sin to obedience, from death to life, from being under the law to being under grace. While some words beginning with *dik* are judicial in Paul, the passive verb seldom is (only in 1 Cor. 4: 4; 6: 11; Rom. 2: 13), and it is the passive verb which bears the brunt of the argument in Galatians 2–3 and Romans 3–4. This is why 'righteousness' by faith is slightly misleading as a summary of Paul's position. The noun 'righteousness' implies a status, while Paul's verb has more the connotation of something which happens to a person. This is seldom legal acquittal. When Paul wrote that he and Peter, though previously not 'Gentile sinners', had been righteoused by faith in Christ (Gal. 2: 15–16), he did not mean that they had been guilty but were now innocent. They had previously been innocent enough, not 'sinners'. When they were 'righteoused' they were made one person with Christ (Gal. 3: 28), or, as Paul put it in another letter, they had become part of a 'new creation' (2 Cor. 5: 17; see 5: 21, 'so that in him we might become the righteousness of God'). The passive of *dikaioun* does not easily bear this meaning—changed, transferred, incorporated into another person—but Paul forced it to do so. The significance of this coercion will occupy us below.

Luther saw the world and the Christian life quite differently.

He was impressed by the fact that, though a Christian, he nevertheless felt himself to be a 'sinner': he suffered from guilt. Paul, however, did not have a guilty conscience. Before his conversion to being an apostle of Christ, he had been, as we saw, 'blameless' with regard to 'righteousness under the law' (Phil. 3: 6). As an apostle, he could not think of anything which would count against himself at the final judgement, though he left open the possibility that God might find some fault (1 Cor. 4: 4). Luther, plagued by guilt, read Paul's passages on 'righteousness by faith' as meaning that God reckoned a Christian to be righteous even though he or she was a sinner. Luther understood 'righteousness' to be judicial, a declaration of innocence, but also fictional, ascribed to Christians 'by mere imputation', since God was merciful. Luther's phrase for the Christian condition was not Paul's 'blameless' or 'without blemish' (for example, 1 Thess. 5: 23), but rather *simul justus et peccator*, 'at the same time righteous and a sinner': 'righteous' in God's sight, but a 'sinner' in everyday experience.

Put another way, Luther saw the Christian life as summed up in Romans 7: 21, 'I find it to be a law that when I want to do right, evil lies close at hand', whereas Paul thought that this was the plight from which people were freed through Christ (Rom. 7: 24; 8: 1–8). 'You', he wrote, 'are not in the Flesh, you are in the Spirit'; and those in the Spirit, he thought, did not do the sinful deeds 'of the Flesh' (Rom. 8: 9–17; Gal. 5: 16–24).

Luther's emphasis on fictional, imputed righteousness, though it has often been shown to be an incorrect interpretation of Paul, has been influential because it corresponds to the sense of sinfulness which many people feel, and which is part and parcel of Western concepts of personhood, with their emphasis on individualism and introspection. Luther sought and found relief from guilt. But Luther's problems were not Paul's, and we misunderstand him if we see him through Luther's eyes.

'Righteoused by faith' in Galatians

To come to grips with the substance of Paul's thought we must first grasp the context of his discussions of being 'righteoused by faith' and then see how he used the phrase. Two parts of the existing Pauline correspondence, Galatians 2–4 and Romans 3–4, are dominated by this concept. They share a common context, and Paul's discussion cannot be understood unless we know the topic that he and his opponents were debating. The subject-matter is not 'how can the individual be righteous in God's sight?', but rather, 'on what grounds can Gentiles participate in the people of God in the last days?'

Numerous passages in the Bible and post-biblical Jewish literature predict that when God establishes his kingdom Gentiles will turn to worship him. Isaiah thought that 'in the latter days' all the Gentiles would come to the temple to worship the God of Israel (Isa. 2: 2). This prophecy of the eschatological pilgrimage of Gentiles does not give legal detail about precisely what the Gentiles should do when they turn to the God of Israel. They are to learn his ways and walk in his path, and the law will go forth from Zion (2: 3), but nevertheless there is no explicit statement that the Gentiles are to become Jews: to accept circumcision, the dietary code, and all the other parts of the Mosaic legislation. All the biblical passages on the inclusion of the Gentiles in the last days are equally vague: they are prophetic or poetic, and they do not specify what worship of the God of Israel entails—except, of course, abandoning the worship of other gods.

Paul, as we saw in the first chapter, set his own work solidly in this context. In Romans 15 he depicts himself as a priest taking the 'offering of the Gentiles', both people and money, to Mount Zion. He took the view that in 'the last days', which had now arrived, the Gentiles should be included *as* Gentiles. They should not become Jews. Neither were they the same as 'God-fearers', Gentiles who were drawn to and supportive of Judaism, since Diaspora synagogues did not require God-fearers to give up the pagan religious rites which were part of civic duty. Paul's Gentile adherents were in a different category: those who forsook idols and turned to the God of Israel in the last days. We call them 'Christian', but that was not yet the standard designation of people who regarded Jesus as Lord. For the sake of convenience, however, I shall continue to call these people, whether Jews or Gentiles, 'Christians'.

It seems that most Jewish Christians who associated with Christian Gentiles agreed with Paul. The church at Antioch, which Paul did not found, did not require Gentile members to become Jews. When the issue arose as a dispute, Paul persuaded the chief Jerusalem apostles that this was correct (Gal. 2: 6–10).

By the sixth decade (whether earlier or not we do not know) some members of the Christian movement disagreed: they thought that Gentiles could not enter the people of God as Gentiles, but that they must become Jewish. Paul's own terms for the Gentile members of his churches could in fact lend themselves to this interpretation: he called them 'descendants of Abraham'. Yet he did not think that they should be forced to become Jewish in the standard way, by accepting the entire Mosaic law, including circumcision for the males.

It should be emphasized that Paul's opponents, when they insisted that Gentile Christians should become Jews, did not oppose the salvation of all people. They held, rather, that Israel knew the will of the one God of the universe, and that the universe should conform to that will, expressed in the law of Moses, though more recently revealed in Christ. Universal salvation, on this understanding, would be achieved by full proselytization to the Jewish messianic sect: acceptance of the election of Israel, the law of Moses, and the saving death of the Messiah Jesus. Paul argued that God required of Gentiles only acceptance of the God of Israel and of Jesus as saviour. The positive term for his position was 'being righteoused by faith', or more fully 'by faith in Jesus Christ', and the negative expression was 'not by works of law' or simply 'not by law'. He applied the requirement of faith in Christ to Jews as well as to Gentiles, as we shall see in Chapter 11, but the argument which produced the phrase 'righteoused by faith' was the basis of Gentile membership in the people of God.

In pursuing the full meaning of these phrases in Galatians, we should distinguish five topics: the autobiographical and personal dimension, which emerges as a narrative about conflicts; the terms in which Paul's opponents argued their position; what Paul's answer was; how he argued for his conclusion; why he had come to it. The distinction between the last two—his arguments on behalf of a position and his actual reasons for holding it—is one that few students or scholars make. Many people will look at the biblical passages that he uses in his arguments and say, 'That gives Paul's reason for his view.' I propose that, while we note the arguments and the use of proof texts, we first analyse all his arguments before deciding what his real reasons were. People often put forward arguments in favour of a position which they reached in a different way.

We take first Paul's autobiographical stories of conflict with other Christians over what should be required of Gentiles: must they keep the Jewish law? In Galatians Paul recounts a series of three confrontations between himself and other Jewish Christians. The first story is that Paul had gone to Jerusalem, accompanied by Titus, a Greek convert and one of his chief aides. 'False brethren' (some Christian Jews in Jerusalem) had wanted to 'force' Titus to be circumcised, but Paul resisted. He reached an agreement with people whom he sarcastically calls the 'pillars' of the Jerusalem church, Peter, James and John. The agreement was that he would continue his mission to Gentiles, that Peter would continue as the chief apostle to Jews, and that Paul's Gentile converts should contribute money to the Jerusalem church (Gal. 2: 1–10).

The second confrontation occurred in the church in Antioch, which was Paul's home base. The church there consisted of both Jewish and Gentile members, who were accustomed to eating together, probably commemorating the Lord's last supper. When Peter came to Antioch he at first joined in. But then James sent a message to him, which resulted in his withdrawal from the Gentiles, and he was followed by the rest of the Jewish members—including even Barnabas, Paul's first apostolic colleague. Paul, at least as he later recalled the story, made an impassioned speech, in which he accused Peter of not behaving in accord with the gospel and of being 'hypocritical'. Having denounced Peter, he then appealed to him, in a passage which we noted above, saying, in effect: 'even though neither one of us started out as a Gentile, that is, a sinner, nevertheless we agree that one is righteoused by faith in Christ, not by works of law' (Gal. 2: 11–21). What specific 'work of the law' triggered this situation is not entirely clear. Perhaps it was the food— Gentile meat and wine, or perhaps it was the company—the chief apostle to the Jews should not associate too much with Gentiles. In any case, the issue was the degree of association between Gentile and Jewish members. If the Jewish Christians would not fully accept Gentiles while they were still Gentiles, they would in effect be attempting to force them to become Jewish, and Paul accused Peter of doing just that (2: 14). We recall that in the first conflict he said that the 'false brethren' wanted to 'force' Titus to be circumcised. Now Peter is accused of the same sort of coercion.

Finally, conflict over the status of Gentile converts arose in Galatia. Christian missionaries had come there after Paul, arguing that the Gentile Christians should become Jewish by accepting circumcision; or, as Paul put it more forcefully, they wanted to 'compel' the Gentiles of Galatia to be circumcised (Gal. 6: 12). This enraged Paul: 'Even if we, or an angel from heaven, should preach to you a gospel contrary to that which we preached to you, let him be accursed!' (1: 8), and it led to the nastiest statement in his letters. He said of his opponents, who wanted the Gentiles to cut off their foreskins, 'Let them cut the whole thing off', which the RSV moderates to 'mutilate themselves' (5: 12).

Whence the passion and rage? Why did they not have a polite academic dispute about the meaning of Isaiah 2: 3? We recall two prime facts about Paul: he was indeed the apostle to the Gentiles, and he fervently believed that his Gentiles were full members of the eschatological people of God. Paul's position was not academic theory; it was a statement of his life's work. When he hurled anathemas at his opponents, and appealed to an apparent agreement with Peter, James and John, he also defended himself as an apostle. His mission and even his sense of self were at stake: 'Paul an apostle—not from men nor through man, but through Jesus Christ and God the Father' (Gal. 1: 1).

To read the letter aright, one must read it as one half of a ferocious debate and imagine the harassed and distraught apostle pacing and dictating, sometimes pleading, sometimes grumbling, but often yelling: 'an apostle *not* from men' (Gal. 1: 1); 'the gospel preached by me is *not* man's gospel' (1: 11); '*nor* was I taught it' (1: 12); 'I did *not* confer with flesh and blood, I did *not* go up to Jerusalem' (1: 16); 'before God, I do *not* lie' (1: 20). Implied in these passages are his enemies' accusation that he was a second-hand apostle and their claim that he should not be followed when he disagreed with the Jerusalem apostles: his assertions about independence were lies.

Similarly with regard to the theological issue, circumcision: 'Titus was *not compelled*' (Gal. 2: 3); 'to *false* brethren we did *not* yield' (2: 4 f.); 'those "of repute" added *nothing* to what I preach' (2: 6). His enemies said that his own aide, Titus, had been circumcised, that Paul had agreed, and that he had conceded to Peter and James that they could decide the issue finally, adding circumcision to the list of requirements if they wished.

The passion and the rage show that Paul the apostle to the Gentiles had to defend both his theology and himself, and his first arguments to the Galatians were autobiographical.

How had his opponents argued their case? The preachers of circumcision held that the God previously accepted only by Israel was God of the world, and that he intended to save the entire world. They viewed Israel's Scriptures as true and as revealing God's will. Thus far, they and Paul agreed. But they wished the Gentile members, in the interim between Jesus' resurrection and his return, to become Jews, and here he baulked. From his answer, which uses the story of Abraham to 'prove' that Gentiles do not need to be circumcised, and from his other defensive statements, we can reconstruct what his enemies had said to the Galatians and (with less certainty) what the latter had replied. This reconstruction is necessary, since their arguments determined the form of Paul's reply, and that, in turn, led to his sometimes curious use of words.

'When Paul was here, did he say that he represents the God of Israel and that Jesus is God's designated Messiah?'

'Yes'.

'Did he say that Jesus' coming was in accord with the Scripture, and that Scripture reveals God's will and intention?'

'Yes, he quoted to us from the Holy Books, and we have begun to study them.'

'Do you know that those who accept Jesus as God's Messiah have committed themselves to obeying the ordinances of God as revealed to Israel in Scripture?'

'Well, Paul did not put it quite that way. But we do see the logic of the position. God sent Jesus and God also inspired the Holy Books, and if we accept one it is certainly reasonable that we accept the other.'

'Have you read Genesis 17 lately?'

'No, copies are a bit scarce, we have not got very far in our study, and we are not sure what you have in mind.'

'Genesis 17 expressly stipulates that all descendants of Abraham—that is, all who follow the ordinances of the God of Israel—are to be circumcised; rather, that the males are to be circumcised. Further, it clearly says that those who are not circumcised will be *cut off* from membership in the covenant between God, Abraham, and his descendants.'

'Well, if that is the case we shall of course be circumcised. We would like a chance to study the matter, and we shall write to Paul to tell him what we are now considering.'

'Did Paul tell you that he is essentially an apostle at one remove? That those who truly know Jesus' gospel are those who followed him in his lifetime and who saw him after the resurrection? That Peter, the chief pillar of the temple of the new age, and the Lord's own brother, James, have priority?'

'No, no, he said nothing like that. We understood that he was invested with full authority to speak directly for God.'

In accordance with this conversation, the Gentile Galatian Christians wrote to Paul or sent a messenger, and he replied by writing what we now have as the Epistle to the Galatians. Since the opponents' argument depended on Scripture, Paul—an expert exegete—replied in kind. He undertook to prove, also from Scripture, that the biblical commandments about being Jewish did not need to be observed by Gentiles in the messianic age. Hence the terms in which the argument was cast: 'descendant of Abraham' became Paul's cipher for 'member of the people of God, one of those who would be saved at the end', and he had to use the language of the Abraham story in order to refute the opponents on their own terms.

When we turn to Paul's answer and mode of argument, we run into the difficult part of his writings, and consequently the difficult part of this book. It should first be emphasized that there is no complexity at all about *what* he thought: he thought that his Gentile converts *must not* be circumcised. So far so good. The difficult parts of the interpreter's task are to explain his complex arguments and to relate his arguments in favour of a position to the actual reason for which he held it. Not all of Paul's arguments, to be sure, are difficult. On the present topic, the circumcision of his Gentile converts, the first argument is autobiographical and depends on his view of the previous conflicts. In the second, Paul argues from experience: 'did you Galatians receive the Spirit when you heard the message and had faith, or when you started observing the Jewish law?' (Gal. 3: 1–5). These are straightforward and easily understandable arguments. It is the third one, based on Genesis, which requires explanation.

Paul argued like an ancient Jew; this is not in the least surprising, though reading the arguments can be bewildering. In Galatians 3: 6–18 Paul argues terminologically, using proof texts from the Abraham story, and making the wording of that story fit his own view. A 'proof text' is a passage from an authoritative source which contains words or phrases that a later author can use to 'prove' his argument, without regard to the original meaning of the passage. Those who know something of modern fundamentalism will understand Paul's technique. He was not concerned with the meaning of biblical passages in their own ancient context. He had in Scripture a vast store of words, and if he could find passages which had the right combination of words, and stick them together, he scored his point. I shall explain this passage in Galatians as an example of scriptural/terminological argument. The technique was a little convoluted, and consequently the explanation is as well. The difficulty with reading Paul, however, is precisely his use of this sort of argument, and it is necessary to look at one example of it.

We begin by knowing the conclusion: Gentile converts to

Christianity are not to be circumcised. Paul wished to prove this by quoting the Bible, and he faced an uphill task, since his Scripture said nothing of the sort, at least not on the surface. The ancient interpreter, however, was prepared to search the text and find the right conclusion.

Paul started his search with the phrase 'descendant of Abraham', almost certainly because Abraham figured prominently in his opponents' argument. According to Genesis 12, God called Abraham to follow him. He made many promises, which are repeated in the following chapters. There was one principal stipulation: God required Abraham and his male descendants to be circumcised (Gen. 17). Paul decided for obvious reasons to ignore chapter 17 and to fix on the story of Abraham's call.

Here he found words which suited his purpose: '[Abraham] had faith in God, and he reckoned it to him as righteousness' (Gen. 15: 6), and 'In you all the Gentiles will be blessed' (Gen. 18: 18). These two verses provided Paul with a total of four words which, when correctly combined, proved his point and led him on to a further argument: faith, righteousness, Gentiles, blessing. He combined the first three into his own statement: 'Scripture said in advance that God *righteouses* the *Gentiles* by *faith*' (3: 8). Paul took this in an exclusivist sense: none of the rest of the story matters, just the bit about Gentiles and faith: that is the only requirement they need fulfil.

He then took up the fourth word, 'blessing'. Its opposite is 'curse', and the two occur together in Genesis 12, where God said to Abraham, 'I will bless those who bless you, and him who curses you I will curse' (12: 3a). Paul, who had just cursed his Jewish Christian opponents, did not want to call down God's curse on people who curse, and thus he used only the word, 'curse', while he went in search of another passage, one which *would* allow him to curse his opponents. He found it: 'Cursed be every one who does not abide by all the things written in the book of the law in order to do them' (Deut. 27: 26, following the Greek which Paul read; the Hebrew has 'does not affirm' rather than 'does not abide by'). This is the only passage in the Greek Old Testament which connects a word for 'curse' with the word 'law' (*nomos*). Since Paul was fighting the application

57

of the law to his Gentiles, here he had his proof text: 'my enemies are cursed, and so are you Galatians if you follow them'. The appearance of the word 'blessing' allowed him to shift from the story of Abraham, which proved his point positively, to the covenantal curse of Deuteronomy, which he hurled at his opponents.

The terminological argument continues, and we shall not trace it in detail, but rather observe two points briefly.

Paul picks up the 'curse' and shows a way out from under it: by hanging on a tree Christ became a 'curse' (Gal. 3: 13). He thus lifts the curse from those who accept him (see below, Chapter 8).

Paul quotes in his favour Habakkuk 2: 4. The passage originally meant that 'the person who is upright will live by trusting God'; Paul takes it to mean that, since 'the righteous lives by faith', 'no one can be righteoused by the law'. That is, he read it as if it said, 'A person is righteoused by faith [only]'. Habakkuk 2: 4 is the only passage in Paul's Scripture, apart from Genesis 15: 6, which combines the terms 'faith' and 'righteousness'.

Although by Galatians 3: 12 Paul has exhausted biblical statements on 'curse' and 'law', and on 'righteousness' and 'faith', the Abraham story has not been exhausted. Paul returns to it in Galatians 4: 21–31, an argument which we shall not analyse, but in chapter 3 he immediately re-uses it. This gives him a term which he can use to make an even grander point than that Gentiles are righteoused by faith [in Christ] and that those who accept the law are accursed. The crucial phrase is 'and to your seed'. Repeatedly in Genesis God tells Abraham that the blessings are for him and his seed (Gen. 12: 7; 13: 15; 17: 7; 24: 7). 'Seed' (*sperma*), Paul notes, is grammatically singular. It is used as a collective noun to mean 'offspring' or 'progeny', and collective nouns, as Paul knew perfectly well, refer to a plurality of individuals. He uses the same passage in its plural sense in Romans 4: 13. For the argument in Galatians 3, however, he insists on the fact that it is singular. The promise was made to Abraham and his *one* seed, who must be the Christ. Here Paul seems to defeat his earlier purpose, which had been to argue that the blessing of Abraham comes upon Gentiles, not just upon one person. He will now play his trump card, which will make the Gentile believers part of the singular seed, Christ, but to play it he must abandon the terms derived from Genesis 15: 6 and 18: 18:

Whoever of you has been baptized into Christ has put on Christ. There is neither Jew nor Greek, there is neither slave nor free person, there is neither male nor female; for you are all one person in Christ Jesus. And if you are Christ's, *then* you are *Abraham's offspring* [*sperma*], heirs according to promise. (Gal. 3: 27–9)

The promise went to Abraham's singular seed, Christ, but other people can be incorporated into Christ and thus inherit the biblical promises to Abraham.

Here Paul combines the experience of the people in Galatia, and what he had preached among them (faith, exemplified in baptism), with the argument based on biblical proof texts. He goes back to the term which stood as a cipher for 'those who will be saved', that is, 'descendants of Abraham'; he insists on the singular 'descendant'; he claims that his Gentile Christians— 'you'—have become part of that singular descendant by baptism into Christ. 'Being righteoused by faith', the key phrase of the earlier terminological argument, has now yielded. By the end of Galatians 3 the status given by faith is not being 'righteoused', but rather that of being a 'son of God' (3: 26). Faith makes the converts 'one person in Christ Jesus'. It is impossible not to see here that 'being baptized', 'putting on Christ', becoming 'one person' with him, and 'being Christ's' are Paul's own terms. He relates them to the biblical terminology, 'descendant of Abraham', by a theory of incorporation which he did not find in his Bible, and for which he had no proof texts, but rather his own thought and experience, and here he uses his own language.

It is often said that to understand Paul's argument the reader must have been thoroughly immersed in the Greek translation of the Hebrew Scripture. Certainly either then or now only the student can fully appreciate Paul's argument. Paul had memorized the Scriptures in Greek, and he could pull out passages which combined certain words; as we have just seen, he cited the only passages which combine 'right-' and 'faith', and the only passage which combines 'curse' and 'law'. The modern reader requires a concordance to learn this, and an ancient would have needed a mastery of the text equal to Paul's. The student can also see just how the passages are combined and linked by word association so as to lead from one point to another. This does not mean, however, that Paul's point can be grasped only by the expert. The Galatian converts, who formerly had worshipped other gods (Gal. 4: 8), could not have recognized just how dazzling was Paul's mastery of ancient exegetical technique, any more than can the ordinary modern reader. They would have seen, though, that Paul had passages in his favour and they saw his conclusions perfectly well. That is, they knew what he wanted and they perceived that he quoted holy writ, just as did his opponents. Paul's argument was aimed not only at his converts but also at his opponents, who quoted Scripture. We need not suppose that the Galatians could follow every nuance of the exchanges between Bible-quoting Jewish experts. They nevertheless got the gist of the argument.

Further, the first verses and the final verses of Galatians 3 appealed to them in other terms. They had received the Spirit apart from the law (3: 1–5); they understood about being baptized into Christ and becoming one person with him (3: 27 f.).

Thus far we do not know *why* Paul thought what he thought. We know what the question was, what his opponents thought, how they argued, what Paul thought, and something of how he argued; but we do not know why he did not agree with them. They had on their side the obvious meaning of Genesis 17. Paul was proud of his Jewish heritage, and he believed in the Scriptures. Why, then, did he not agree?

I think that we can get at the question by considering two other passages in Galatians and related material. One is that Paul writes, surprisingly, that 'neither circumcision nor uncircumcision is anything, but a new creation' (Gal. 6: 15). This is important to Paul. He wrote it in his own hand, and it is an appeal for agreement. That neither circumcision nor uncircumcision matters is found in other passages: 'For in Christ Jesus neither circumcision nor uncircumcision is of any avail, but faith working through love' (Gal. 5: 6), and 'Neither circumcision counts for anything, nor uncircumcision, but keeping the commandments of God. Everyone should remain in the state in which he was called' (1 Cor. 7: 19–20).

Similarly, in Romans 14 Paul characterizes as matters of indifference two other important parts of the Jewish law: the dietary laws and the observance of 'the day' (the sabbath). In this chapter these are laws which one may or may not keep; the only requirement is sincerity of purpose. Yet in the heart of Galatians, these same three points—circumcision, eating together, and keeping days—touched off rage, curses, appeals and tortured argumentation. How could they also be unimportant or matters of indifference?

Paul's different attitudes towards circumcision and the other main signs of obedience to the Jewish law must have depended on the significance which was attached to them *by others*. His own attitude could be either this or that, depending on the circumstances. I shall return to reconstructing the positions of others. Let us suppose that one of Paul's converts spoke to him as follows:

'Paul, I have long been attracted to the Jewish way of life, and I responded to your preaching because I was persuaded that Jesus was indeed the promised Anointed One of Israel. Now that I have been baptized and have become a member of the body of Christ, I know that I am *truly* a descendant of Abraham. I am now motivated, though, to complete my commitment to the God of Israel by becoming an Israelite, and I wish to undergo circumcision and to accept the major points of Jewish law. Since you are Jewish, this would make me also a closer imitator of you, who are my father in the faith.'

Paul, I imagine, would have replied,

'This is not in any way a necessary step. God intends to bring Gentiles to salvation precisely *as* Gentiles. Further, the time is short, and I would have everyone remain in the same state. There is no point in becoming Jewish, any more than in divorcing or marrying. None of these things matters. However, if you wish circumcision, it does you no harm, except for the minor and temporary pain, and I see no objection to your following your own desire. Just be sure that you are circumcised to the glory of the Lord, not to gratify those who are "of the flesh".'

This imaginary reply draws on Galatians 5: 6; 6: 15; 1 Corinthians 7: 19 and Romans 14.

Let us now imagine another conversation. Someone from Jerusalem, let us say one of the original disciples—not Peter or John, but one of the lesser figures—comes to Paul and says this:

'Paul, you are deceiving those Gentiles. Jesus—had you known him— would never have approved. He did not preach to Gentiles, but sought only to restore the lost sheep of Israel. He referred to Gentiles as 'dogs' (Mark 7: 27). They are all right, of course, if they convert, if they accept circumcision and so inherit the promises to Abraham; that is, if they accept the Mosaic ordinances, live upright lives and remain in that way faithful members of God's covenant with his chosen people. They must fix their faith on Jesus as God's anointed messiah, to be sure, but when he returns he will distinguish the sheep from the goats, and those who do not observe the law given to Moses by the same Holy One who sent Jesus will not be saved. What you are saying to them destroys their only hope; they become persuaded by you that they will inherit the promises to Abraham when they do not even *begin* to keep God's covenant with him, the sign of which is circumcision.

Further, not only is your message completely false, you have no rights in this matter anyway. All you know about Jesus you heard second hand. Your supposed gospel is no gospel, and your supposed apostleship is no apostleship. You are a pseudo-apostle, preaching a Jesus who is not recognized by those who actually knew him.'

We have seen Paul's response to this in Galatians 1–2. He rants, curses his opponents, justifies his own apostleship by appealing to direct revelation, and argues that any of his converts who accept the view of his enemies will be cut off from Christ.

Study of the three instances of the verb 'to compel' or 'to force' in Galatians will reveal why Paul sometimes held that circumcision and days *must not* be accepted. 'False brethren' in Jerusalem wanted to 'force' Titus to be circumcised; Paul accused Peter of trying to 'force' the Gentile Christians to live like Jews; he claimed that his opponents in Galatia were trying to 'force' the Galatians to be circumcised. When people said, 'You *must* become Jewish by accepting circumcision, food laws, and days', Paul replied, 'Those who accept circumcision will be cut off'. If instead one asked a question, 'Paul, what about circumcision?', the answer was, 'In and of itself it does not matter.'

We can and should put these two answers together: Since circumcision does not matter, it must not be treated as if it does; Gentiles must not be forced to be circumcised. Why not? Because, if circumcision were necessary to salvation, salvation would come by being Jewish. Christ's death would not have been necessary. As Paul puts this argument, 'if righteousness were through the law, then Christ died in vain' (Gal. 2: 21).

This was the theological side. Personally for Paul, victory by those who wished to 'compel' Gentiles to be circumcised would mean that his mission had been in vain. He should not have converted and become apostle to the Gentiles. He should have remained a good Pharisee, trying to make others obey the law, persecuting them if they did not.

In other words, the reason for which Paul took the view which we have seen is that it was tied up with his theological conviction that God sent Christ to save the world by his death and resurrection, and with Paul's personal conviction that he had been called to convert the Gentiles. The sending of Christ and the call of Paul would not have been necessary if salvation came by being Jewish. Since God had taken these steps, they *were* necessary. Therefore it was not necessary to be Jewish, and those who thought that Gentiles must become Jews were to be cursed. If Gentiles accepted this, they would be renouncing the death of Christ, which Paul had 'placarded' before their eyes, when they accepted the gospel by faith and received the Spirit (Gal. 3: 1–5).

'Being righteoused by faith in Christ not by works of law', then, in Galatians means substantively that Gentiles who have faith in Christ do not need to become Jewish and that even those who are already Jews in good standing are rightly related to God only by their faith in Christ (see especially 2: 15). To express these simple propositions Paul fired barrage after barrage, employing an extraordinarily wide range of terms. The argument which concludes chapter 3 provides a good example: Those who are *in Christ*, who are *baptized into him*, are *Abraham's offspring*. Abraham was the recipient to God's promises, and the way to become a co-recipient is to become *one person in Christ Jesus*. These other terms do not mean something different from being 'righteoused by faith'. The terminological variation springs from the different proof texts which Paul used: 'righteoused by faith' comes from Genesis 18: 18 and 12: 3, and 'Abraham's offspring' or 'seed' comes from such passages as Genesis 12: 7. To these he added his own terms.

At this stage, we shall not try to determine more closely what Paul 'really meant': the religious reality which lies behind his terminological argument. Subsequently, however, we shall recall that at the end of Galatians 3 he makes use of phrases which are not derived from proof texts.

With regard to the Jewish law, we do not yet see a full and nuanced treatment. The negatives are clear: one is not righteoused by keeping the law; the inheritance (of the promises to Abraham) is not by the law (Gal. 3: 18); the law cannot make alive (3: 21); those under the law are enslaved (4: 5–9; 4: 21–31). All of these are simply the negative versions of Paul's positive statements: one is righteoused by faith in Christ, those in Christ inherit the promises made to Abraham, Christ brings freedom and (implicitly) life. Yet in arguing that one is not righteoused by the law, Paul quotes the law as containing valid statements: it is the Jewish law which provides his proof texts. Further, he favours the fulfilment of the law which is summed up by Leviticus 19: 18, 'you shall love your neighbour as yourself' (Gal. 5: 14). One of the main works of the law, circumcision, which at one point is said to 'sever' a believer from Christ (5: 4), at another is said not to matter (6: 15). The reader of Galatians can only guess at how to hold these positions together, and they will occupy us in Chapter 9.

7 Righteousness by faith and being in Christ: Romans

Paul was not under direct attack when he wrote Romans, and the letter is much less polemical than is Galatians. He had also listened to criticism of his position and had thought some more about the issues. The church at Rome was not of his founding, and this too affected the tone of the letter. He could berate the Galatians and threaten them, or appeal to their initial response to him and play on past sympathy and warmth (for example, Gal. 4: 14f.). These persuasive devices were not appropriate when writing to a church that was not his own, but others were. He was not too proud to use compliments when urging the Romans to hear him out:

I long to see you, that I may impart to you some spiritual gift to strengthen you, that is, *that we may be mutually encouraged* by each other's faith, both yours and mine. (Rom. 1: 11f.)

Late in the letter, looking back on his admonitions, he softened them by a flattering disclaimer: the Roman Christians were already full of both goodness and knowledge, but ... (15: 14). He certainly thought that he had the right to instruct them, but he was conscious that he must not claim authority over them.

The criticism which Paul takes into account in Romans was that his attack on the Jewish law might lead to immorality, since the law, among other things, served as a guide to human behaviour. After writing that the law has the function of increasing trespass, or making it worse, and assuring the readers that 'where sin increased, grace abounded all the more', he must now caution against immorality: 'Are we to continue in sin that grace may abound? By no means!' (5: 20–6: 1). A few verses later he asks, 'Are we to sin because we are not under law but under grace?', and makes the same denial: 'By no means!' (6: 15). That he himself had been accused of undermining morality is explicit in 3: 8: 'And why not do evil that good may come?—

as some people slanderously charge us with saying.' This accusation helped push him to some very strong statements in favour of the law: 'Do we then overthrow the law by this faith? By no means! On the contrary, we uphold the law' (3: 31; cf. 7: 7, 12 f.). This has no counterpart in Galatians.

Despite such differences between Romans and Galatians, the discussion of 'being righteoused by faith' is substantially the same. The problem is, again, that of Gentile inclusion in the people of God. The single most important theme of Romans is equality of Jew and Gentile.

the gospel ... is the power of God for salvation of every one who has faith, to the Jew first and also to the Greek. (Rom. 1: 16)

There will be tribulation and distress for every human being who does evil, the Jew first and also the Greek, but glory and honour and peace for every one who does good, the Jew first and also the Greek. For God shows no partiality. (2: 9–11)

Are we Jews any better off? No, not at all; for I have already charged that all people, both Jews and Greeks, are under the power of sin. (3: 9)

For there is no distinction ... (3: 22)

Or is God the God of Jews only? Is he not the God of Gentiles also? (3: 29)

[God makes known] the riches of his glory ... [for] us whom he has called, not from the Jews only but also from the Gentiles. (9: 23 f.)

For there is no distinction between Jew and Greek; the same Lord is Lord of all and bestows his riches upon all who call upon him. (10: 12)

For God has consigned all people to disobedience, that he may have mercy upon all. (11: 32)

As the climax to the first part of this argument (Rom. 1–3), Paul asserts that all, whether Jew or Gentile, are equally righteoused by faith (3: 30), and again, in chapter 4, he turns to the story of Abraham to prove the point. This time he implicitly acknowledges Genesis 17, according to which God said to Abraham that he and his offspring must be circumcised. Paul now points out that God pronounced Abraham to be righteoused *before* he required him to be circumcised. Thus Abraham stands as both 'the father of all who faith without being circumcised' and also 'the father of the circumcised who are not merely circumcised but also follow the example of the faith which our father Abraham had before he was circumcised' (4: 11–12).

In the discussion in Romans 3–4 the verb 'reckon' (*logizomai*), derived from Genesis 15: 6, comes into prominence (3: 28, and eleven times in chapter 4). This does not mean, however, that Paul thinks of righteousness as being fictitiously imputed to those who have faith, while they remain sinners in fact. In sharing Christ's death Christians have died to the old order. They no longer live in sin (6: 2), but are 'slaves' of righteousness, who have become obedient to God (6: 15–18). Paul picked up 'reckon' from Genesis, and then he repeated it, with no thought of a fictional, 'merely imputed' righteousness.

As the argument about the equal status of Jew and Gentile in the people of God rolls on, it is combined with Paul's concern about ethics and the law. In Romans 6, as we saw above, he wishes to refute the idea that Christians, being free from the law, sin so that grace may abound (6: 1 f.), and he tries to explain how, without the law, ethics are maintained. He argues that Christians, being 'in the Spirit', are able to put to death evil deeds and to fulfil what the law requires (8: 1–14). In chapters 1–3 Paul had argued that Jews and Gentiles alike sinned, and in chapters 3–4 that membership in the people of God had been made available to Jew and Gentile equally. Now he argues that Gentiles are on the same footing as Jews with regard to doing what is right: those who die with Christ (6: 5–11) and live in the Spirit do what is pleasing to God (8: 8).

In this argument (chapters 6–8) the phrase 'righteoused by faith' recedes in favour of other sets of terms. That God 'righteouses' is repeated in Romans 8: 30, 33, where the discussion is judicial: God righteouses rather than condemns (8: 33). That the person who dies with Christ is 'righteoused' from sin—that is, freed from it—is stated in 6: 7. Nevertheless the thrust of the argument in chapters 6–8 is conveyed by other terms: dying with Christ (6: 5–11), being set free from sin (6: 18), dying to the law or the Flesh (7: 1–6), being in Christ Jesus (8: 1), and being in the Spirit rather than in the Flesh (8: 9). As we saw in Galatians, these are not different from 'being righteoused';

rather, they say the same thing in other words. But when Paul leaves behind his scriptural arguments, which are based on the Abraham story, he also, for the most part, leaves behind the terminology which is connected with it.

We have now surveyed most of the passages which make the interpretation of Paul difficult and contentious. Those about the law have been quickly passed over, and we shall return to them in Chapter 9. Now we should concentrate on the interpretation of 'being righteoused by faith', 'being in Christ Jesus', 'dying with Christ' and related phrases.

The main lines of what Paul thought about the two major issues which are in view in Galatians and much of Romans can be stated quite simply:

Membership: Paul held that faith in Christ was the sole requirement for membership in the group of those who would be saved. Negatively, this meant that accepting the Jewish law was not necessary. This is the meaning of 'righteoused by faith in Christ, not by works of law' and similar phrases.

Behaviour: Christians should live morally blameless lives. The idea of fictional, imputed righteousness had not occurred to him, but had it done so he would have raged against it. We shall consider his moral perfectionism in Chapter 10.

Since Paul is sometimes thought to be hopelessly difficult to understand, we should emphasize that his views about two of the major concerns of any religion are straightforward and simple. 'Who counts as a member of the in-group?' and 'How should members act?' are the two practical questions with which religion must deal. (Most other major questions are speculative: Whence do we come? What happens after death?) To the two practical questions Paul replies: All who have faith in Christ, with no further distinctions of any kind, are members. They should act perfectly.

Despite the basic simplicity of these two answers, there are difficulties within each point. To see the complications with regard to membership, we may ask two questions: What terminology best expresses Paul's real thought? When a person becomes a member, what changes—the person or God's opinion about that person? These questions overlap, and answering one helps us answer the other. We begin with the second.

A change at work in the world

One of Paul's most striking views is that those in Christ had already begun the process of transformation which would culminate at the return of the Lord. Sometimes, in fact, he wrote as if the change had already taken place: 'If any one is in Christ, he is a new creation; the old has passed away, behold, the new has come' (2 Cor. 5: 17).

This is, however, overstatement by Paul's usual standard. In Romans, although he puts 'death with Christ' in the past tense, he stops short of putting resurrection with Christ into the past: 'We were buried therefore with him by baptism into death, so that as Christ was raised from the dead by the glory of the Father, we too might walk in newness of life' (Rom. 6: 4).

One would have expected, 'As Christ was raised ... we too have been raised'. 'Walk in newness of life' implies that the full transformation comes at the return of the Lord or the resurrection. In Romans 8: 19–25 Paul makes clear the relationship between what Christians already have and what is to come. In the present age, the whole creation awaits liberation from bondage. Christians have the 'first fruits' of the Spirit, but we still await full adoption as 'sons', which means 'the redemption of our bodies'. On the basis of such passages one might think that the only changes, in Paul's view, were in God's attitude towards the individual, and in the individual's outlook and mental orientation. He held, however, an intermediate position between 'the new creation has already arrived' and 'only attitudinal changes have taken place'.

And we all, with unveiled face, reflecting the glory of the Lord, are being changed into his likeness from one degree of glory to another; for this comes from the Lord who is the Spirit. (2 Cor. 3: 18)

Though our outer nature is wasting away, our inner nature is being renewed every day. (2 Cor. 4: 16)

Here the verbs are in the present passive: the Christian is being changed. In the first passage, the change 'from one glory to another' (the word 'degree' does not appear in Greek) recalls 1 Cor. 15: 40. There are heavenly bodies and there are earthly bodies; 'the glory of the heavenly is one, and the glory of the earthly is another'. According to 2 Corinthians 3: 18, then, Christians are in the process of being changed from one to the other. They will end up with a body like Christ's after the resurrection, a 'spiritual body' (1 Cor. 15: 44, 48 f.).

How realistically did Paul think of a transformation in the present? This sort of question is one of the hardest to face the modern student of an ancient thinker. Today most people draw a sharp line between 'physical' and 'mental, emotional or spiritual', a line which our view of 'laws of nature' makes almost absolute. Either the body is being changed, in which case we should be able to observe and measure the change, or the only change is that of mental outlook and orientation—either physical or psychological. Paul too could distinguish between inner–spiritual and outer–physical, and he does so in the passages we have cited. Yet his view was not just the same as ours. 'There is one glory of the sun, and another glory of the moon, and another glory of the stars; for star differs from star in glory' (1 Cor. 15: 41). To us, these are all physical entities, and we know that they are composed of the same basic elements. To Paul there was a continuum, from one glory to another, and he used these different glories as an analogy for the change of individuals from earthly glory to heavenly glory. One was not less 'real' than another, just as the sun is not less real than the moon or the earth. He himself had *seen* the risen Christ, 'the man of heaven', to whose image Christians were in the process of being transformed (1 Cor. 9: 1; 15: 46 f.). He knew that the risen Lord did not have a 'natural' body, but a 'spiritual' one (1 Cor. 15: 44); nevertheless it could be seen.

Could the transformation of Christians be seen? Paul realized that it could not. The bodies of the believers, whether living or dead, would be transformed only at the return of the Lord (1 Cor. 15: 51; Rom. 8: 23; 2 Cor. 5: 1 f.). The only sign of change perceptible to the five senses of the observer was the 'wasting away' of the 'outer nature' (2 Cor. 4: 16). This may be connected to Paul's view that Christians had to suffer to be like Christ and to be transformed into his image (Rom. 8: 17). Whether suffering is the meaning of 'wasting away' or not, we may take it that Paul could not point to progressive signs of glorification which were visible to the observer. This does not, however, mean that his statement that Christians were 'being changed' is only a figure of speech for moral redirection.

We can best see this by focusing directly on ethics and noting the degree to which Paul thought that correct behaviour was the inevitable consequence of becoming one person with Christ: a member of Christ's body lived accordingly, naturally producing the 'fruit of the Spirit'. Paul seems not to have spent his time in each city teaching ethics. We find him having to give elementary ethical admonition by letter, and he seldom appeals to the readers to remember what he had told them when present. The apparent explanation of this strange fact is that he thought that correct behaviour was the consequence of baptism and that deeds related to people as fruit to trees.

The converts seem to have thought so too. One of them, probably inspired by the proclamation, 'You are a new creation', thought that he could therefore take up sexual relations with his stepmother (1 Cor. 5: 1–5); the relationships of the old world had passed away, the new had come, as Paul himself maintained (2 Cor. 5: 17; and see further pp. 106 f. below). Paul was horrified and shocked. He and the Corinthian agreed that those who were members of a new order had been transformed; they disagreed on what this meant. The Corinthian correspondence shows how realistically some or all of Paul's converts understood the change which he proclaimed; they really were new people (cf. 1 Cor. 4: 8). When we add this realism to the fact that in his correspondence Paul often gives very basic ethical instruction on major issues, with no indication that he had given it before, we must conclude that he and his converts thought that their membership in the body of Christ really changed them, so that they would live accordingly. He thought that his converts were dead to sin, alive to God, that conduct flowed naturally from people, and that it varied according to

71

who they really were. Those who were under sin *naturally* committed sins: 'those who are *in* the Flesh *cannot* please God' (Rom. 8: 8); those who were in Christ produced 'the fruit of the Spirit' (Gal. 5: 22).

This 'realistic' view of human transformation and of behaviour as the natural product of each sort of person may be contrasted with the psychological explanation of how Paul's ethics related to his basic proclamation of salvation. According to this model, Paul preached 'righteousness by faith' as imputed. Converts accepted their own ineradicable sinfulness, but they were psychologically freed by the proclamation that God nevertheless considered them innocent or righteous. Since the gospel made them feel that they were loved, they were then able to love one another, on the perfectly sound principle that love begets love. Those who are emotionally secure are able to deal more generously with others than can those who are emotionally deprived.

What is wrong with this is that Paul wrote nothing of the sort. As we shall see more fully in Chapter 10, Paul's ethical admonitions are not connected to the 'doctrine' of righteousness by faith, but principally to two other conceptions: being a member of the body of Christ and being in the Spirit. Both of these relate to who a person is and in what higher power he or she participates, not to self-perception or mental or emotional outlook. For people today, the psychological explanation works quite well, while the realistic one is hard to grasp. It was otherwise for Paul and his readers.

If it be granted that, in Paul's view, membership in the body of Christ changed believers in some real sense, rather than just changing their perception of God and the world, we may still ask whether God's opinion of them also changed. The answer is yes. Paul did not, to our knowledge, discuss ledgers on which God recorded the names of the righteous and the wicked, but he did think that God kept track of who was who. At the return of the Lord, some would be transformed to be like him, but others would be destroyed (Phil. 3: 18–20).

It is more important, however, to note that Paul thought that God did something other than keep track of people and alter his opinion about them. God 'righteoused' the person of faith as well as 'reckoned' the person to be righteous. The active verb, with God as subject, occurs in Romans 3: 26, 30; 4: 5; 8: 30, 33; Galatians 3: 8. The usual formulation is the passive verb; a person 'is righteoused'. This passive, however, implies God as the understood subject: 'a person is righteoused by God'. This means not just that the person's name was moved from one side of God's ledger to another, as 'reckon' might imply, but that the person was transferred to another sphere, called variously 'the body of Christ', the Spirit, and the like. In this transfer a real change was effected, the first step towards the glorified body which would be attained at the return of the Lord. As a result of this change the new person found that good deeds flowed out naturally and that everything which the law had required was 'fulfilled' in his or her life (Rom. 8: 4).

These last sentences, on their own, give too mechanistic a view. Paul did not think that Christians or others were automatons. He knew full well that his followers could make decisions and act according to them, and he exhorted them to do the deeds of the Spirit: exhortation implies the ability of those exhorted to make their own decisions (for example, Gal. 5: 16). Paul did not explain how he could maintain both that one person cannot obey God, while another does so naturally (Rom. 7: 15–23; 8: 7 f.), *and* that at each individual point people could choose. The Corinthian church member did not have to live with his stepmother (1 Cor. 5: 1–5), Christians could choose whether or not to employ prostitutes (1 Cor. 6: 15–20), and so on, through the whole range of behaviour. Just as Paul, in common with other first-century Jews, did not see that there is a logical problem in holding together God's providence and human choice (Ch. 5), he also did not see that the theory of natural 'fruit' does not harmonize well with the idea of free choice. Each statement—the law is fulfilled in Christians, non-Christians cannot please God, people can choose whether to obey God's will or not—reflects something which was deeply meaningful to Paul and which he held without secondary rationalization of how it fitted in with everything else he thought.

In this chapter I have been especially concerned to explore

the aspect of Paul's thought about membership in the body of Christ which people today tend to overlook. This is not only, however, as a curiosity from the ancient world, but also because it puts us in touch with the depth of Paul's thought and of his faith in God. He thought that God could actually change the most intractable part of the creation—humanity.

The central terminology

We have already, in effect, answered the question of which set or sets of terminology reveal the most important parts of Paul's thought: those which depict actual change by participation in a new creation, rather than those which are judicial or legal.

Paul believed in God the judge, and thus he also believed in decrees of guilt or innocence. We have previously noted instances in which the verb 'to righteous' or 'to be righteoused' is legal (Rom. 2: 13; 8: 30, 33; 1 Cor. 4: 4; 6: 11). There are other judicial passages. In Romans 5: 18–21 the opposite of *dikaiōsis*, rightness or acquittal, is 'condemnation'. That the Christian, though assured of salvation, must still be judged for transgression is explicitly stated in 2 Corinthians 5: 10.

Despite all this, the deeper levels of Paul's thought are not found in the judicial categories, but in those which express the participation of the faithful in Christ or in the Spirit, a participation which produces a real change. There are several observations which justify this conclusion.

In the first place, in both Galatians and Romans Paul leaves behind the language of 'being righteoused', with its possible judicial construal, when he moves away from his proof texts. In Galatians 3 the first proof texts lead him to talk about being righteoused by faith. He then shifts, however, to the question of who are the descendants of Abraham, and his answer to this is that people who are in Christ are Abraham's descendants. Similarly he largely drops the language of being righteoused after Romans 5 in favour of speaking about dying with Christ (Rom. 6: 5–11), becoming a slave of righteousness or of God (6: 18, 22), dying with Christ (again) and thus belonging to him (7: 4), being in Christ Jesus (8: 1), and having Christ or the Spirit of

God indwelling (8: 9–11). His own language tells us more about how he thought than does the language of his proof texts.

Secondly, some of the principal judicial passages are derived from previous Christian tradition. The identification of pre-Pauline formulas in Paul's letters is not a completely certain science, but scholars generally agree that Romans 3: 21–6 is entirely or partially pre-Pauline, as is 1 Corinthians 6: 9–11. Again, Paul's own terms tell us better how his mind worked.

Thirdly, the judicial line of thought treats Christ's death as a sacrifice which wipes out transgressions (for example, Rom. 5: 18). All agree, including those who think that the legal categories are central to Paul, that this is not his own most characteristic view of the death of Christ. That we see in such passages as Romans 6 and 2 Corinthians 5: 14 f.: 'he died for all; *therefore all have died*'. His distinctive view of the death of Christ is that it provides the believer with a way of escape from the old creation by sharing Christ's death (Chapter 8, below).

Fourthly, Paul forces the etymologically judicial word 'righteoused', which should be 'declared innocent', to mean 'transferred from one state to another', 'becoming part of the body of Christ'. We saw above the clearest case of coercion of meaning: in Romans 6: 7 the perfect passive verb 'one who has been righteoused' is forced to mean 'one who by dying with Christ escapes the old creation where sin reigns'. But throughout Galatians 2 and 3 'to be righteoused' means that the person who has faith in Christ is shifted from the old being to the new being. When Paul wrote that he himself, though a good Jew, was 'righteoused' only by faith in Christ (Gal. 2: 15–16), he meant that he had been 'crucified with Christ', with the result that it was no longer he who lived, but Christ who lived in him (2: 20). The coercion of language reveals its real meaning. 'Being righteoused' means 'dying with Christ' and sharing his life.

Fifthly, most of Paul's ethical discussions have to do with the behaviour of one who is a member of the body of Christ (1 Cor. 6: 15 f.; 10: 1–22), or who is a participant in the Spirit or in Christ (Rom. 8: 2–11). Paul's ethics are organically related not to legal innocence, being declared to be righteous, but to participation in another being or power.

Finally, we note that the judicial category is terminologically defective. We do not find the word 'guilt' at all, which is the legal counterpart on the human side of God's condemnation, and the words 'repent(ance)' and 'forgive(ness)' are virtually absent ('forgiven' appears only in an Old Testament quotation in Romans 4: 7). These terms, central to any scheme of judicial decision about guilt and innocence, play virtually no role in Paul's discussion of 'being righteoused by faith' or of becoming Christian. To a degree the judicial categories work *within* Christianity. Christians would have to answer for their deeds at the judgement (1 Cor. 3: 15; 4: 4; 2 Cor. 5: 10), and Paul expected people who were already Christians to repent of improper behaviour (2 Cor. 7: 9 f.; 12: 21). This implies that they could be forgiven. What is striking is that these categories, well known to any good Jew, play no role in the argument about 'being righteoused', since that has to do with the question, 'Who are in the people of God?'. The way to get in, and the definition of those who remain in, are better stated by Paul when he writes about dying with Christ and being one person with him.

Another way of putting all this is to say that 'righteoused by faith' means 'being transferred from the group which will be destroyed to that which will be saved'. This transfer involves a change in the person, so that Christ lives in and through the believer. The deeper meaning of Paul's difficult passive verb, 'be righteoused', is that one dies with Christ and becomes a new person.

8 Christology

What did Paul think of the person whom God had chosen to save the entire world, the man with whom Christians became one? Paul says little about Jesus directly and quotes his words only a few times. He knew that Jesus was 'born of woman, born under the law' (Gal. 4: 4) and that he was 'descended from David according to the flesh' (Rom. 1: 3). Yet, though he had once done so, he determined no longer to regard Christ 'according to the flesh' (2 Cor. 5: 16). He was the Son of God.

It may be helpful if we make a distinction with regard to Christ which would later be made in classical Christian theology. There are two aspects to 'Christology': the person of Christ and the work of Christ, that is, who he was and what he did. In the third, fourth, and fifth centuries a lot of effort was expended on statements of who he was, but the creeds and other Christological formulations of those centuries, which are still accepted throughout Christianity, are largely negative, in that what they forbid is clearer than what they permit. A doctrine of the work of Christ was never achieved, and one can speak only of theories of the atonement. Christians agree that Christ 'saves' in some way or other, but not necessarily on how he does it.

Both of these two aspects of Christology emerge in Paul's letters, though, of course, without the formal terms and definitions of later centuries. Paul's discussions of 'the work' of Christ are more rewarding, since he had obviously given them more thought, and we begin with them.

How Christ saves

There are two streams of thought in Paul with regard to how Christ benefits the believer. Neither includes discussion of what the historical Jesus did and said. One, rather, is an interpretation of the significance of his death, while the other fixes on both death and resurrection.

In the first place, Jesus' death was sacrificial. Sacrifices were part and parcel of ancient religion, including Judaism. There were many reasons for sacrifice, but a major one was the expiation of sin. In an expiatory sacrifice the blood which is shed is regarded as wiping out a transgression. Thus, for example, Leviticus appoints a 'guilt offering' to be brought to the temple by anyone who has done 'any of the things which the Lord has commanded not to be done', whether or not the transgressor committed the offence knowingly (Lev. 5: 17–19). The logic of atonement—why sacrifices erase transgression—is not clear in Leviticus, but one possible explanation of how they work is that the animal dies as a substitute for the human transgressor. This idea has many modern parallels. Soldiers who die in war can be understood as dying on behalf of non-combatants and in their stead. In *A Tale of Two Cities* Sydney Carton dies in place of Charles Darnay.

According to 1 Corinthians 15: 3, 'Christ died for our sins', that is, to atone for them. In Romans 3: 25 expiation is 'by his blood', and according to 4: 25 he was 'put to death for our trespasses'. When Paul writes that 'we are righteoused by his blood' in Romans 5: 9 he is thinking of the expiation of transgressions, as is clear in 5: 18, where 'one man's act of righteousness', which leads to acquittal, refers to Jesus' death. Substitutionary thinking is seen in Galatians 3: 13: he 'became a curse for us', which means 'in our stead' as well as 'on our behalf'. In 2 Corinthians 5: 21 Paul writes that 'for our sake [God] made him to be sin who knew no sin'. When the sinless one was made 'sin' and then died, he took the place of others. This idea probably lies behind Romans 8: 3.

Some of these passages are parts of pre-Pauline formulas. This is explicit in 1 Corinthians 15: 3 ('I delivered to you as of first importance *what I also received*'), probable in Romans 3: 21–5, and possible in Romans 4: 25. The very earliest Christians interpreted Jesus' death as atoning, and Paul accepted this understanding.

It has, however, been generally recognized that the sacrificial interpretation of Jesus' death does not lie at the heart of Paul's thought. W. D. Davies put it this way: 'Although in labouring to do justice to the significance of the Death of Jesus he uses sacrificial terms, Paul does not develop these but leaves them inchoate.' This view is common to numerous scholars of diverse schools of interpretation, and here the scholarly consensus is correct.

When Jesus' death is regarded as sacrificial, the human problem which it overcomes is perceived as *transgression*. People commit wrong actions, for which they require forgiveness or acquittal. Acquittal, in turn, requires the shedding of blood. We have seen throughout, however, that Paul has a more radical conception of sin than that it is transgression. Humans are not just sinners, they are enslaved by a power: Sin. Repentance and acquittal of individual transgressions do not fully meet the human problem. People are not just guilty, they are enslaved, and they need to escape. Paul thought that the power of Sin was so great that one must die to be free of it, and accordingly he reinterpreted Christ's death. People who become one person with Christ share his death and thus escape bondage, and they then share his life, being freed from the power of Sin. Herein lies Paul's distinctive contribution to thought about the death of Christ.

If we live, we live to the Lord, and if we die, we die to the Lord; so then, whether we live or whether we die, we are the Lord's. For to this end Christ died and lived again, that he might be Lord both of the dead and of the living. (Rom. 14: 8f.)

What matters is belonging to Christ, and his death makes this possible. The 'mechanics' of the transfer from being under Sin to living in the Spirit are spelled out in a passage which we have often cited, Romans 6: 5–11. When people die with Christ they escape bondage to Sin: 'death no longer has dominion over us' (6: 9b). This is repeated in Romans 7: 4–6:

Likewise, my brethren, you have died to the law through the body of Christ, so that you may belong to another, to him who has been raised from the dead in order that we may bear fruit for God. While we were living in the Flesh, our sinful passions, aroused by the law, were at work in our members to bear fruit for death. But now we are discharged from the law, dead to that which held us captive, so that we serve not under the old written code but in the new life of the Spirit.

According to 2 Corinthians 5: 14 Christ 'died for all' with the result that 'all have died'. This echoes a line from Paul's earliest surviving letter: he 'died for us so that whether we wake or sleep we might live with him' (1 Thess. 5: 10). Christ gave himself 'for our sins' not only in order to accomplish their acquittal but, more, 'to deliver us from the present evil age' (Gal. 1: 4).

Here again we see that, although Paul knew and employed forensic or judicial ideas (sin is transgression; God acquits those who have faith in Christ; his death wipes the slate clean), the heart of his thought lies in another set of ideas: participation in Christ and a change of one's state from being under Sin to living in the Spirit. The death and resurrection enable the person who has faith in Christ to make this change, by sharing the transfer which was first made by him.

The person of Christ

Here Christianity did eventually come up with a doctrine. It may help us to understand two passages in Paul's letters if we briefly note the problem of later Christology. The positive statement is that Christ was completely human and completely divine. As we pointed out above, this was defined negatively. In him humanity and divinity were neither discrete nor combined. This means, for example, that one may not say that the divine person performed miracles, since one may not separate divinity and humanity. Nor may one say that only the human half suffered. A 'half and half' Christology is excluded by the creeds. It is equally heretical to regard him as a third entity, neither quite human nor divine. In practice people have to choose which heresy they commit (to overstate the matter only slightly), denial of true divinity or of true humanity. Liberal Christians have generally tried to redefine true divinity so as not to interfere with humanity, which is for them more important. Conservatives often give only lip service to true humanity in order to preserve divinity. They may propose, for example, that one should not study the historical Jesus by using the ordinary methods of criticism, since he was not an ordinary person. The Christological statements of the creeds pose difficulties for people who wish to remain within what they permit, but nevertheless to talk about Jesus.

Paul, of course, did not see the problem in these terms; on the contrary, he seems not to have known that there was a problem. He thought that all those who were under the law were enslaved by Sin, that Jesus was 'born of woman, born under the law' (Gal. 4: 4), and yet that he had not known sin (2 Cor. 5: 21). This is one of the numerous instances in which he did not write his views down on one sheet of paper, and thus did not ask himself how to hold them together.

The two most substantial passages in which he commented on who Jesus was are Romans 1: 1–6 and Philippians 2: 5–11. In the first passage he states that Jesus was 'descended from David according to the flesh and designated Son of God in power according to the Spirit of holiness by his resurrection from the dead' (Rom. 1: 3 f.). The reader of this passage would understand that Jesus was 'designated' Son of God, and further that he was designated such only at the time of the resurrection. In later terminology, this is an 'adoptionist' Christology. Jesus was adopted by God as Son, not born that way.

The second passage goes to the other extreme. According to Philippians 2: 5–11, Jesus was 'in the form of God' before he was born, but then he took on 'the form of a slave, being born in the likeness of men'. The passage continues, 'and being found in human form he humbled himself and became obedient unto death'. God 'highly exalted him and bestowed on him the name which is above every name', that is, Lord. Here, strikingly, the word 'Son' does not appear. Instead one gets 'form': Jesus was in the form of God, then he was in the form of a slave, that is, he was in human form. By emphasizing 'form', one might argue that Paul is saying that Jesus was neither truly divine nor truly human, he was only in the form of each successively. This, however, would be to pick at words. Whatever the complexities of the wording, the passage basically states that Jesus Christ was pre-existent and was in some sense divine, but that he became human before being exalted even higher than he had originally been, to the status 'Lord'.

One sees that it is impossible to derive from Paul's letters anything approaching one single doctrine of the person of Jesus Christ. It is possible that both the passages just quoted are pre-Pauline in origin, in which case they show that he drew on, rather than composed, quite diverse statements, one offering a 'low' Christology, the other a 'high' Christology.

Though these passages do not constitute a harmonious point of view, considering them allows us to see from another angle Paul's fundamental conviction, which was that in Christ *God* acted to save humanity. It is quite easy to overlook the importance for Paul of *theo*logy in the narrow sense, but once one spots it, it crops up everywhere. We saw earlier, in Chapter 5, the great Jewish doctrine that whatever happens was intended by God and serves his purpose. Now we may see the great Christian doctrine that in Christ God *somehow or other* acted to save the world. The most famous passage is 2 Corinthians 5: 19, 'in Christ God was reconciling the world to himself'. This is Paul's view of the 'work of Christ', that it was God acting through him, to save the world.

That Christology is a handmaid of theology is seen most clearly if we return to the question of the work of Christ and note that besides the views that his death atones for sin and that it provides the possibility of death and renewal for the person who is 'in' him, there is a third function: the cosmic.

Then comes the end, when [Christ] delivers the kingdom to God the Father after destroying every rule and every authority and power. For he must reign until he has put all his enemies under his feet. The last enemy to be destroyed is death. (1 Cor. 15: 24–6; cf. Rom. 8: 18–39)

God not only used Christ to effect a transfer from the old to the new life for those who have faith in him in this world, he also will use him to bring about the destruction of all the powers of darkness. It was God who planned the great scheme of salvation history seen in Romans 9–11: both Jew and Gentile were locked up in sin; Christ was sent by God in order that he, God, could have mercy on all. Just how it worked is stated in different ways, but here we have the great conviction of Paul's life and theology: in Christ God acted to save the entire world. How would he do it, given humanity's reluctance? Paul answered, in effect: 'Trust him, he is God, he knows what he is doing.'

9 The law

We have already seen a lot of the Jewish law. Paul sometimes sounds as if it is the polar opposite of the new revelation in Christ. One is righteoused by faith in Christ, not by the law. Yet this does not tell the whole story. Paul by no means took an unambiguously negative stance towards his heritage.

The two pillars of common Judaism were the election of Israel and the giving of the law. This is revealed in a curious way in Paul's letters, where their importance is seen in the amount of difficulty they caused. We have previously mentioned the fundamental theological problem that Paul faced: how to reconcile the old dispensation and the new, both of which he believed in. The law received especially tortured and tortuous treatment, and we shall now take it up in more detail.

A surface difficulty in understanding Paul on the law is that he wrote different things about it, depending on circumstances. We have already glimpsed this. If someone said to one of his Gentile converts, 'You must be circumcised', Paul would reply that accepting circumcision meant renunciation of Christ. Yet if the subject were posed differently, Paul could maintain that neither circumcision nor uncircumcision mattered: it did not matter provided that no one thought it did. As was his view of circumcision, all of the diverse things which he said about the law were determined by circumstances. This should cause neither amazement nor alarm. It does not mean that Paul had no organizing principles or that his statements were simply random. Each thing that he said about the law was consistent with one of his major principles. He did not have, however, one single theology of the law. It was not the starting point of his thought, and it is impossible to give one central statement about the law which explains all his other statements. It is quite possible, however, to explain each of the various things which he wrote about it. We shall discuss four contexts in which the law figures; the third is the one which reveals his fundamental theological problem.

The law as membership requirement

There is little more to be said about the law when Paul debated requirements for membership in the people of God. The statement that one is 'righteoused by faith not by law' means that one does not 'die with Christ' by observing the law; on the contrary, in Christ Christians die to the old world, of which the law is a part (for example, Rom. 7: 4–6).

The question of Paul and the law starts becoming more complicated when we note that he has both more positive things to say about it and also much more negative things than that it does not righteous. He claims that he 'upholds' the law (Rom. 3: 31), he favours keeping the commandments (1 Cor. 7: 19; Rom. 13: 8–10; 8: 4; Gal. 5: 14), and he states that 'the law is holy, and the commandment is holy and just and good' (Rom. 7: 12); yet he virtually equates the law with Sin and the Flesh (Rom. 6: 14; 7: 5 f.), and he maintains that the purpose of the law is to provoke sin or to condemn all of humanity (Gal. 3: 19, 22; Rom. 3: 20; 4: 15; 5: 20).

The law and correct behaviour

The positive statements are relatively easy to understand: for the most part he agrees with the behaviour which the law requires. In Galatians, as he neared the end of his argument against circumcision, he saw the need to address the question of how Christians should behave. Christians are free, and in particular free from observing the law; yet this should not lead to abuse. They should love one another, as the law said—'Love your neighbour as yourself.' This fulfils 'the whole law' (Gal. 5: 14, quoting Lev. 19: 18). In Romans 13 Paul states that 'the one who loves the neighbour has fulfilled the law', and he then lists four of the ten commandments: the prohibitions of adultery, murder, theft and covetousness (Rom. 13: 8–10). In Romans 8 he claims that in Christians the requirement of the law is 'fulfilled' (Rom. 8: 4).

What the law requires is good (Rom. 7: 12). As apostle, Paul continued to hold his native view on this point with relatively little systematic reflection. We shall see in Chapter 10 that he generally supposed that Jewish practice, especially when it conflicted with pagan, was correct. Yet we have also seen that he sometimes opposed circumcision and the sabbath. How can we understand his embrace of 'the whole law' if he did not accept parts of it?

Some New Testament scholars have tried to analyse the law to see which parts are not caught by the commandment 'Love your neighbour'. They have focused on something which they call the ritual law as being excluded: Paul kept the moral law but opposed the ritual or cultic. This is not an ancient Jewish categorization of the law. Paul did not invent it, nor would he have agreed with it, as we shall see below. We can make better progress if we briefly consider how ancient Jews did categorize the law.

They commonly distinguished two categories of commandments, those which governed relations between humans and God and those which governed relations among humans. If this distinction is made, Leviticus 19: 18 is a summary of the 'second table' of the law, the laws which govern relations among humans. Any attentive reader of Leviticus would see this; this verse summarizes the preceding ones, which require Jewish farmers to leave food in the fields for the poor and which prohibit theft, robbery, lying, oppression, and cheating. Although Jews sometimes cited Leviticus 19: 18 as a summary or epitome of this 'second table', more often it was used as a summary of 'the law' in general. It was also turned into an epigram: 'What you hate, do not do to anyone.' The epigram is found in Tobit 4: 15, and it is attributed to the Pharisee Hillel in the Babylonian Talmud (Shabbath 31a). Philo wrote that 'what a person would hate to suffer he/she must not do to others' (*Hypothetica* 7: 6). Paul uses the negative epitome at the end of his summary of the law in Romans 13: 10: 'Love does *no wrong* to a neighbour, therefore love is the fulfilling of the law.'

Those who used the negative epitome did not think that it had only negative implications. Philo followed his epitome, 'do *not* do', with positive illustrations, such as, 'If the poor or a cripple beg food of him, he must give it as an offering to God' (*Hypothetica* 7: 6). Similarly when Paul summarized the law by quoting prohibitions and using the negative epitome he did not intend to limit 'the law' or 'love' to prohibitions of evil. In 1 Corinthians 13 he gives a positive account of actions which spring from love.

Nor did people who cited 'love your neighbour' or 'do not do wrong to others' as summarizing the entire law intend to exclude the other table, the laws between humans and God. Philo firmly believed in sacrifice, as did Tobit and Hillel. Jesus provides an even more striking example. According to one passage, when he was asked about the chief commandments, he offered two: 'love God' (Deut. 6: 4) and 'love your neighbour' (Lev. 19: 18). These are the best summary passages of the two tables. Yet he could also epitomize 'the law and the prophets' by saying, 'whatever you wish that people would do to you, do so to them' (Matt. 7: 12). Logically, this statement includes only one half of the law, yet Jesus did not reject the other half. He approved of sacrifice for both atonement (Matt. 5: 23 f.) and purification (Mark 1: 44).

Efforts to summarize are not logical exercises. They are attempts to catch the spirit of the law. This applies both to Paul and to other Jews of his time.

When we examine Paul's letters in more detail, we see that he by no means excluded all the commandments on the 'first table'. On it stand these laws.

> You shall have no other gods before me.
> You shall not make for yourself a graven image.
> You shall not take the name of the Lord your God in vain.
> Observe the sabbath day. (Exod. 20: 2–11; Deut. 5: 7–15)

Most of these Paul accepted; the exception is the sabbath day. He objected to the Galatians' observing the holy days of the

87

Jewish calendar (Gal. 4), and he wrote to the Romans that keeping days was optional (Rom. 14). He doubtless opposed 'days' in Galatia because his enemies had introduced them. He may very well have kept the sabbath himself, while opposing efforts to make it mandatory for Gentiles. In any case his negative attitude towards 'days' in Galatians does not allow us to say simply that he was against the sabbath, since he considers it optional in Romans 14.

Of more interest in considering Paul's attitude towards the commandments which govern relations between humans and God are the first two commandments: 'You shall have no other gods before me' and 'You shall not make for yourself a graven image ... you shall not bow down to them or serve them.' Paul lived in a world which was teeming with images of gods and in which they were elaborately 'served' with sacrifices and feasts. Since he was apostle to the Gentiles, former pagans, he had to sort out his attitude towards these two commandments.

The question was raised by the Corinthians. Could they eat meat which had been offered to an idol? In the ancient world animals generally did double duty: people sacrificed them to a god and then ate them. In the pagan Mediterranean some meat from a sacrificed animal might end up in the public market. Paul's reaction is most instructive. He instinctively drew back from a practice which was abhorrent to Jews, and he brought forward two arguments against it. One was that participation in an idol's cult and in the Christian eucharist are mutually exclusive:

Shun the worship of idols ... The cup of blessing which we bless, is it not participation in the blood of Christ? ... I do not want you to be participants with demons. You cannot drink the cup of the Lord and the cup of demons. You cannot partake of the table of the Lord and the table of demons. (1 Cor. 10: 14–21)

This upholds the biblical commandment not to 'serve' other gods by worshipping in their temples—in this case, worshipping by participating in a sacrificial meal, shared among the worshippers, the priests, and the altar. Yet Paul argues the case not by quoting the second commandment, but by appealing to a new principle: participation in the blood of Christ. Those who share the Lord's supper must not be contaminated by sharing a demon's meal. One sentence in this passage relies on the Mosaic code: 'what pagans sacrifice they offer to demons and not to God' (1 Cor. 10: 20), which echoes 'they sacrificed to demons which were no gods' (Deut. 32: 17). Yet Paul does not quote the commandment itself.

Two chapters earlier Paul had offered another argument against eating meat derived from idolatry. If a 'strong' person, who knows that idols have no real existence, eats meat offered to one, a 'weak' Christian might stumble, since the weak person might think that the strong person was actually worshipping the idol. 'If food is a cause of my brother's falling, I will never eat meat, lest I cause my brother to fall' (1 Cor. 8: 9–13). This argument is, in effect, an effort to bring a 'cultic' law under the commandment, 'Love your neighbour'. Paul was not opposed to the cultic part of the law as such, though he had an aversion to quoting commandments. He intended 'Love your neighbour' to be an epitome of the whole law as it applied to behaviour, whether 'ethical' or not.

The Corinthians had argued in favour of eating idolatrous meat by appealing to what Paul had taught them. They knew that 'an idol has no real existence', and consequently that what had been offered to idols was offered to nothing. Paul had to grant that they were right (1 Cor. 8: 1–6). Finally, he partially yielded to their argument. Though they could not worship at a temple, his converts could eat what was sold in the market or what they were offered when guests of another, unless the source of the meat was explicitly said to be sacrifice (10: 23–30).

Formally, Paul held that his Gentile converts were free from the law, a principle which made him reluctant simply to quote commandments to determine behaviour. Yet his own views of proper behaviour, both 'ethical' and 'cultic', were Jewish to the core. In 1 Corinthians 8 and 10 we see him wrestling with his converts, trying to work out proper behaviour on the basis of beliefs which they shared, without quoting the laws of Exodus and Deuteronomy. They believed that there was only one God and that only he should be worshipped by sacrifice or any other means—agreeing with the contents of the 'first table' of the Mosaic commandments. They believed that they should take no action which would be injurious to another—agreeing with Leviticus 19: 18, 'Love your neighbour'. Finally, they believed that they were united in the body of Christ and that this union imposed certain behavioural constraints. Using these principles, Paul and his Gentile followers tried to work out what was right and wrong, and they did this in matters which related both to fellow humans and to God.

A final point will allow us to complete consideration of Paul's attitude to the first table of the Jewish commandments. 'Do not *serve* other gods' (Exod. 20: 5) meant, to the ancients, do not sacrifice to them, and it implied that one should sacrifice to the one God. Paul did not oppose the implied commandment to sacrifice: among the blessings which God gave to Israel was service (RSV 'worship'), that is, the temple cult (Rom. 9: 4).

He did not, then, oppose the first table as such: only the sabbath law was optional. He seems not to have sat down, written a list of laws on the first table, and said, 'I am against those'. Nor does he seem to have made any other lists so as to define theoretically which laws he favoured and which he opposed or held not to be necessary. With the aid of hindsight, however, we can now supply a heading for the laws which he opposed in Galatians and which he either opposed or held to be optional elsewhere: those which, in the Diaspora, separated Jew from Gentile: circumcision, rules governing eating, and observance of the sabbath ('days'). Further, these were the points of the Jewish law which most often drew negative comments from Gentile authors. Apart from those points where it separates Jew and Gentile, the law reveals God's will, including correct behaviour. Thus when Paul wished to give a quick summary of proper Christian behaviour he could fall back on the standard epitome which he had learned as a child.

We shall turn to other aspects of behaviour in the next chapter, where we shall see further how Paul applied the commandment to love thy neighbour, and also how his Jewish inheritance sometimes was in conflict with the views of the Gentile members

Dunn

of his churches. Thus far we have seen only part of what he meant when he said that Christians should keep the 'whole law'. In fact, he rejected some of it—not, as many have proposed, using anachronistic terms, the 'cultic' or 'ritual' law, nor, using those of his own day, 'the commandments which govern relations between humans and God'. He rejected, rather, the aspects of the law which were against his own mission, those which separated Jew from Gentile in the people of God. Once he excluded circumcision, food, and days from 'the commandments of God' (an exclusion which is explicit with regard to circumcision in 1 Cor. 7: 19), he could say, without contradicting himself, that his followers should observe 'the whole law': they should accept it after he redefined it. This is not immediately clear, since he revised the law on an *ad hoc* basis, without offering theoretical principles for deleting part of the law which God had given. Consequently, this part of his thought has always troubled readers. Redefinition, however, is the common currency of religious thinkers who use inherited traditions and texts. It is the next topic which is truly difficult, and he was conscious of the difficulty. Thus the contradictions pointed out by Räisänen

The purpose of the law

We saw earlier, in Chapter 5, that one of Paul's major and unquestioned assumptions, an assumption common to Jews, was that God controls history and that consequently whatever happens accords with his will. Paul believed that God had chosen Israel and given them his law. Thus he had to ask why he had done so, since the new revelation which had come to him had meant that being Jewish and accepting the law was not a formal requirement for those whom God would save. What, then, had been the law's purpose in God's plan for humanity? Paul probably once had thought that God had given it for life and that it had potentially offered life: those who were loyal to it would be saved. We see the remnant of this view in Romans 7: 10: the commandment promised life. His new view, however, was that life came to those who died with Christ. Since God intended all humanity to be saved by faith in Christ, it had to follow that he had not intended to save people by giving the law. Yet he had given it.

Paul's bold, even shocking, answer to this problem we saw briefly in Chapter 5: God gave the law in order to condemn, with the ultimate purpose of saving people through Christ. This first appears in Galatians 3: 19: 'Why then the law? It was added because of transgressions, till the offspring should come to whom the promise had been made.' He continued:

The law was our custodian [*paidagōgos*] until Christ came, that we might be righteoused by faith. But now that faith has come, we are no longer under a custodian; for in Christ Jesus you are all sons of God, through faith. (Gal. 3: 24–6)

Without context, these statements might mean that the law was given to restrain transgressions and that it served as *pedagogue* (leader of a child) in the sense of preparing people for the coming saviour. In Galatians 4: 1, however, the child is said to be 'no better than a slave': the child was not trained by the law, but enslaved by it. 'Added because of transgressions', means 'added in order to produce transgressions' or 'to condemn them', not 'restrain them'. This giving of the law had in view the ultimate purpose of God, 'that we might be righteoused by faith'. 'That' in this sentence (3: 24) is a purpose clause, 'in order that' (Greek, *hina*), which here as in several other places in Paul's letters points to God's ultimate aim, to save all by faith in Christ. Earlier Paul had written that those under the law are under a curse '*in order that* the blessing of Abraham would come upon the Gentiles' (3: 10–14). Galatians 3: 22 is clearer yet: 'the scripture consigned all things to sin, *in order that* what was promised to faith in Jesus Christ might be given to those who have faith'. God intended to condemn by the law because he intended to save everyone in another way.

Paul makes similar statements in Romans: no one will be righteoused by the law, 'since through the law comes knowledge of sin' (3: 20); 'the law brings wrath, but where there is no law there is no transgression' (4: 15); the law entered human history 'to increase the trespass' (5: 20).

In all these cases the law is positively connected with sin and condemnation *by God's own will*. The strength of this theology is that it attributes everything that has happened to God's will, in general accord with Jewish monotheism, while maintaining that even bad things were intended by God as preliminary to salvation.

On the other hand, since this view assigns sin and condemnation directly to God's will, it opens the way to criticism of God as not always willing the good. It is understandable that Paul offered alternative positions with regard to God's purpose in giving the law.

In Romans 7: 7–13 he explains that 'the law is holy, and the commandment is holy and just and good', and that the commandment promised 'life' but nevertheless 'proved to be death'. Sin used the commandment 'you shall not covet' to create covetousness. The recipient of the commandment would not have known about covetousness at all had it not been forbidden. The prohibition brought knowledge of covetousness and thus gave opportunity for Sin to go to work.

In this explanation, God's intention was not to condemn. That was the by-product of the commandment, though a by-product in which another power, Sin, played a creative role. Paul seems not to have been entirely happy with this explanation either. Perhaps he perceived that positing an alien power, outside of God's control, which could use good to create bad, led to theological problems (see p. 38 f. above, on dualism).

For whatever reason, he proceeds immediately to another explanation (Rom. 7: 14–25). The law is good (as in 7: 7–13), but people are not able to obey it because their physical bodies contain another law which forces them to do things they do not want, and prevents them from doing the good which the law requires.

This is another form of dualism: anthropological dualism. The theory of a good mind or soul in an evil or weak physical body was widely known in the first century, and here Paul makes one of his rare uses of it. Anthropological dualism denies the goodness of the created order, and thus again leads to an accusation against God or to the view that the creator God is not the same as the good God. That is, anthropological dualism can readily lead to theological dualism, and in any case it denies a cardinal theological belief of Judaism: that God created the world and pronounced it good (Gen. 1: 31).

Paul had a problem, as does every monotheist who contemplates the existence of evil, especially Jewish monotheists, who have usually maintained that God controls history. Paul, however, was not an abstract theologian, and he may not have faced the problem of evil very fully before he became apostle to the Gentiles. The form in which it struck him was not the general question, 'How can there be evil in a world created and controlled by a good God?', but the specific issue, 'How does the old dispensation relate to the new?' That is: if the one God, who is good, controls history, and has now decided to send his Son to save all alike, whether Jew or Gentile, provided that they have faith in him, *what in the world was he up to when he gave the law?* Paul's major explanation—which, however, he retracted in two different ways in Romans 7—was that the law was given to condemn. His alternatives to this involved him in one kind of dualism or another.

It is important to note that after Romans 7 he returns to the first explanation, though without explicit reference to the law. In Romans 8: 19 f. he states that God subjected the creation to futility, planning to redeem it later. In Romans 11: 32 he states that God 'consigned all people to disobedience, *in order that* he could have mercy on all'. It seems that, when all was said and done, Paul preferred to maintain the doctrine of God's providence: whatever happens, including sin and disobedience, happens by his will.

We saw above that this did not mean that humans were not free moral agents (cf. pp. 71–3). Stoics believed in fate or destiny, and the more sophisticated attempted to face the question of how to reconcile fate with individual human choice. Paul was no philosopher. When he thought about God, he naturally regarded him as omnipotent. When he thought about humans, he naturally thought of them as able to make decisions.

We now see the full force of the statement that Paul did not have one theology of the law. He had a problem in reconciling the two dispensations: the old, represented by Moses, and the new, given in Christ. His most basic instinct was to relate them by having the old lead up to the new negatively: the law condemned so that God subsequently could save through Christ. We have seen that this had the advantage of attributing to God a consistent purpose. We have also seen that retractions of it led him into one form of dualism or another, that is, into other sets of theological problems. Saying that Sin seized the law from God was to say, in effect, that God's purpose failed; Sin overpowered or outfoxed him. Saying that humans, being creatures of flesh, could not obey the law was to say, in effect, that God made a bad job of creating them.

Now we should note an answer that Paul seems not to have thought of at all: God changed his mind. At first he intended to save people by giving them the law, but he re-thought the issue, retracted the law, and made a second effort. This would mean that God had not always intended to save by faith in Christ. Such a view would have reduced Christ to the role of an expedient, one which might itself be superseded, and it would have made God whimsical. The Homeric stories attributed whim to the Greek gods, and this was one of the reasons they had to be interpreted by allegory. A god who does first one thing and then another, with no consistent purpose, was not regarded as a worthy god by thinking pagans, much less by Jews. Paul thus instinctively sought a single master plan which encompassed both the Mosaic law and Christ.

Romans 7 has often been viewed as the keystone of Pauline theology. Rudolf Bultmann, the most influential New Testament scholar of the first half of the twentieth century, treated it as such, and this view of the chapter went hand-in-glove with the view that anthropology was central to Paul: he had a fixed view of the nature of humanity, and his theological views were a reflex of this anthropology. We shall not explain and criticize Bultmann's position, but in view of the long popularity of the view that Romans 7 is the most important chapter for understanding Paul, several further comments about it will be in order.

The specific commandment which Paul discusses is the

prohibition of covetousness. It is this commandment which, in 7: 7–13, Sin seizes and uses to create covetousness. The same commandment is probably in view in 7: 14–25, when Paul complains that 'I do not do the good I want, but the evil I do not want is what I do' (7: 19). It has been recently observed that, of the major Jewish commandments, only the prohibition of covetousness could be employed to make these points. One could not say, of the prohibition of murder, that the commandment taught people what murder is, and thus led each person to murder, since most people do not commit murder. The same comment applies to all the other prohibitions in the ten commandments. All deal with things which are avoidable and which many people successfully avoid. Covetousness is the only 'internal' transgression, or, more accurately, the one which most readily can be internalized. In the context of the ten commandments 'you shall not covet' means 'you shall not do anything to acquire what you covet by dishonest means'. But the wording, 'do not covet', lends itself to understanding the prohibition as meaning 'do not covet in your heart'. That, Paul could honestly say, can hardly be avoided. The commandments prohibiting murder and theft, however, can readily be observed.

This simple but insightful comment leads to the conclusion that Romans 7 does not represent a complete analysis of humans and how they relate to commandments. It can hardly stand at the centre of Paul's negative statements about the law. It is too partial an analysis.

The second comment is an attempt to explain why in Romans 7 Paul retracted his view that God gave the law in order to condemn. We have thus far said that attributing this intention to God was problematic, since it assigns transgression directly to his will. It appears, however, that this became a problem for Paul only because of the argument which begins in Romans 6. In Romans 3, 4, and 5 Paul had repeated without hesitation the view that God intended the law to create and then condemn transgression. In Romans 6 and the first verses of Romans 7, however, the law becomes more and more connected with Sin itself. The old world, to which the believer dies with Christ, was one governed both by Sin and by the law. 'For *Sin* will have no dominion over you, since you are not under *law* but under grace' (6: 14). Here the two are virtually equated. According to Romans 7: 4 the Christian dies 'to the law', just as to Sin and the Flesh. This virtual equation was so marked that Paul had to ask the direct question, 'Is the law sin?' (7: 7). In effect, he had just said so; but when he went that far down this path he was forced to back up, and then he began to retract the equation. The retractions of Romans 7 seem to have been triggered by the momentum of the argument, which had finally gone beyond making the law the agent of condemnation and had made it part of the old order, almost equivalent to Sin, Death, and the Flesh.

When we see that 7: 7–25 is a retraction of an exaggeration of Paul's first view—that the law was given to condemn—and that he subsequently reasserts the same theological viewpoint (God himself subjected the creation to futility and God himself consigned all people to disobedience (Rom. 8: 19f.; 11: 32)) we also see that Romans 7 is not the centre of Paul's thought.

Finally, to complete consideration of this chapter we must ask one of the oldest and most discussed questions about it: who is the 'I' who speaks? Is it Paul the Christian apostle who says of himself, 'I do not do what I want, but I do the very thing I hate' (verse 15)? or Paul speaking of his own pre-Christian life? or does the 'I' represent humanity in general? What is clearest is that the Christian life, or at least Paul's perception of it, is depicted in Romans 8: here, Christians are not in the Flesh but in the Spirit (8: 9), and they do the deeds of the Spirit. What the law requires 'is fulfilled' in them (8: 4). They are thus distinguished from the 'I' of Romans 7.

Nor is the 'I' Paul before he became apostle. *That* Paul was 'blameless' with regard to righteousness under the law (Phil. 3: 6). Further, the 'I' of Romans 7, as we saw, faces a grossly exaggerated situation. It was not autobiographically true of Paul that he could do only what was evil (7: 19), nor was it true of anyone else. The unavoidable character of sin in Romans 7, we noted, has to do only with the commandment 'do not covet'. Most people avoided other major transgressions, just as most succeeded in doing many things which were right. Thus this is not a true description of Paul's pre-Christian life, nor of the non-Christian life of humanity in general. It may be that a lot of people feel that way some of the time, but it is neither an accurate analysis of the human condition nor a description of standard human psychology.

Romans 7, in other words, does not actually describe anyone, except possibly the neurotic. Why, then, is it there? The cry of anguish is probably a cry of theological difficulty. The problem, as Paul saw it, was that in Israel's past God had given the law but had not sent Christ; and true fulfilment of what the law requires, he thought, comes only to those who are in Christ, or in whom the Spirit of Christ dwells. It is only in this theological sense that Paul could maintain that one cannot do the law. If by theological definition only those in Christ escape condemnation because they fulfil the law (cf. Rom. 8: 1–4), then by theological exaggeration Paul could say that non-Christians cannot do what is right (7: 18 f.; 8: 7 f.). Just as his view of Christian perfection did not correspond to empirical observation (see Chapter 10), neither did the theory that those outside of Christ were completely unable to do what the law requires. Yet his black and white theology—*either* in and good *or* out and wicked— forced him into this position. In Romans 7 he laments on behalf of those whom his own theology placed completely outside the will of God. Further, he was full of anxiety as he faced the possibility that God could be charged with injustice. He had given the law long ago; salvation comes only through Christ, and thus the God-given law, again according to Paul's own theology, serves only to condemn. These aspects of his theology are probably the factors that led to the anguished cry on behalf of those 'under the law' but not 'in the Spirit'.

Comparison of the old dispensation and the new

We should now very briefly note that there is a fourth context in which Paul mentions the law, that of direct comparison between the dispensation of law and the dispensation of faith in Christ. There are two such passages, 2 Corinthians 3 and Philippians 3: 3–11. According to the first, the old dispensation was 'glorious', or a dispensation of 'splendour', but the new dispensation is much more glorious. In comparison with the new, the old dispensation turns out 'to have no splendour at all, because of the splendour that surpasses it' (2 Cor. 3: 10). According to the second passage, Paul himself had once had 'righteousness under the law' (Phil. 3: 6), and this counted as 'gain'. But this gain he came to consider 'as loss for the sake of Christ' (3: 7).

In both these passages, the law is not actually bad, but rather the old dispensation as a whole is worthless in view of the new. Here too Paul offers a view of the law which is quite different from Romans 6, according to which the law was virtually the same as Sin. We see that this is hyperbolic. If put with better nuance, the law is not Sin, but rather is worthless in comparison with salvation through Christ.

How Paul thought

In Chapter 5 we noted that a person who believes in God's providence is inclined to read history 'backwards'. He or she starts with the outcome; since God intended the outcome, what went before must have happened to lead up to it. The revelatory moment, through which Paul read history, was his own commission to be apostle to the Gentiles when God revealed his Son to him (Gal. 1: 16). The only conclusion that Paul could draw from this revelation was that God intended to save the world, Jew and Gentile alike, by faith in Christ. Since this was so, the law had not been given for 'life' or 'righteousness'. If righteousness were by the law, Christ had died for no reason, in vain (as he explicitly says, Gal. 2: 21). But Christ evidently had not died in vain: he, Paul, had seen him (1 Cor. 9: 1). Therefore, the law had never been intended to bring righteousness (Gal. 3: 21).

This is a theological, in fact dogmatic view. Held as a fixed conclusion, it forced him to readjust everything else he thought. He thought that all, Jew and Gentile alike, must have needed the newly revealed salvation. He therefore described them as heinous sinners (Rom. 1–2). That description did not rest on empirical observation, nor did he arrive inductively at the conclusion that all are under Sin. Thus the fact that it is exaggerated does not really shake his conclusion, since the conclusion was the reflex of his opening dogmatic view: the conclusion that all are under Sin is as sound as the dogma that all need to be saved by faith in Christ.

Similarly with regard to the law. He had not done psychiatric case studies of covetous people and learned that they coveted only because they heard the commandment not to covet. Nor had psychological study led him to the view that attempting to obey commandments leads to self-alienation. The critique of the law is not experiential but again theological or dogmatic. The law must do something bad, since it was not intended by God to save—since God saves through Christ.

This view of the law, however, was a problem for him. We may safely assume that he had grown up loving the law, and that he had regarded it as God's great gift to Israel. It did not come easy to him to turn it into an agent of condemnation rather than one of atonement and grace. Harder and more agonizing yet was what his theology forced him to say about God's election of the Jewish people. We shall turn to that problem in the final chapter. First, however, we shall examine in more detail how Paul dealt with questions of behaviour. This will reveal more illustrations of how he both upheld the law and maintained that Christians were not under it, and it also enables us to assess various cultural influences on him and his churches.

10 Behaviour

While they waited for the return of the Lord, Paul's converts were to behave uprightly, maintaining moral perfection:

May the God of peace himself sanctify you wholly; and may your spirit and soul and body be kept sound and blameless at the coming of our Lord Jesus Christ. (1 Thess. 5: 23)

... so that you may approve what is excellent, and may be pure and blameless for the day of Christ. (Phil. 1: 10)

Similar admonitions are found in 1 Thessalonians 3: 13; 4: 3–7; Philippians 2: 15; 2 Corinthians 12: 21; Romans 6: 19; 16: 19. Guided by Luther, many scholars overlook Paul's perfectionism, but this partial list of passages shows that it was an appreciable aspect of his preaching.

Much of Paul's theology is autobiographical, and this is especially clear in his treatment of behaviour. He himself did not do things half-heartedly. As a Pharisee he had been blameless with regard to the law (Phil. 3: 6), and while an apostle he lived 'devoutly, righteously and blamelessly' (1 Thess. 2: 10; cf. 1 Cor. 4: 4). The moral perfection which he required of his converts, he first required of himself. This came all the easier because he expected the end to come soon. Christians, he thought, should not be too entangled in the world, since 'the appointed time has grown very short' (1 Cor. 7: 29–31). His failure to devise a repair-system for transgression probably reflects his expectations of perfection and of the return of the Lord.

Thus, urged on partly by his own strictness and perfectionism, partly by the view that the time was short and that absolute uprightness could be maintained in the interim, Paul admonished his converts, encouraged them, occasionally praised them for their behaviour—and was sometimes horrified by it.

Effort and fruit

Just as Paul saw himself as exemplifying the correct behaviour, so also he saw himself as the model of exertion:

You remember our labour and toil, brethren; we worked night and day, that we might not burden any of you, while we preached to you the gospel of God. (1 Thess. 2: 9)

Effort characterized not only his manual labour to support himself (so also 1 Cor. 4: 12), but also his activity as an apostle: he worked harder than any of the other apostles (1 Cor. 15: 10; 2 Cor. 6: 5; 11: 23, 27), and he dreaded the thought that he might have laboured in vain (1 Thess. 3: 5; Gal. 4: 11; Phil. 2: 16). He had special respect for other leaders of the new movement who worked hard: 1 Thess. 5: 12; 1 Cor. 16: 16; Rom. 16: 6, 12. Paul fully espoused and observed a 'work-ethic', as long as the goal was the right one. His opposition to 'works of the law' was not motivated by dislike of effort.

He expected his converts, following him and his 'fellow workers' (Phil. 2: 25; 4: 3 and often elsewhere), to labour at 'the work of the Lord', trusting that it would not be in vain (1 Cor. 15: 58). God would see to it that faithful work had good results (1 Cor. 3: 6), and it would be rewarded; but those who did not build with the best materials would be punished (1 Cor. 3: 13–15; 4: 4; cf. 2 Cor. 5: 10). Paul rejoiced at learning of the 'work of faith and labour of love' on the part of the Thessalonians (1 Thess. 1: 3). He knew that they had exhibited love of 'the brethren', but still he urged them to try harder: 'do so more and more' (1 Thess. 4: 10). He instructed the Corinthians to 'pursue' love (1 Cor. 14: 1); sometimes he used the simple imperative, 'love' (Gal. 5: 14; cf. Rom. 13: 8).

Paul also thought, however, that good deeds should flow naturally from life in Christ. In Romans 8: 4 the wording is strikingly passive: 'that the just requirement of the law might *be fulfilled* in us'. Paul, it is to be remembered, thought that people who were in Christ were 'a new creation' and that they lived in the Spirit. More strongly, they had become one person in Christ Jesus. Paul prayed that his converts would 'be pure and blameless for the day of Christ, *filled with the fruits of righteousness which come through Jesus Christ*' (Phil. 1: 10–11). The fruit, then, was not really theirs, but Christ's; and they were a part of Christ. The theory of participation in Christ helps explain Paul's perfectionism and gives it a theoretical basis: Christians should bear such fruit and only such fruit. He did not, however, regard effort in doing good as being in any way opposed to membership in the body of Christ.

Generalities, misunderstanding, and further advice

During the founding visits to each city Paul probably couched instruction about behaviour in general terms. Writing to Thessalonica, he recalled that when there he had 'exhorted', 'encouraged' and 'charged' his converts 'to lead a life worthy of God' (1 Thess. 1: 11–12). We may be certain that he always advised love, especially love of fellow Christians (1 Thess. 4: 10; Gal. 5: 13; 6: 10), and that he urged his hearers to live by the Spirit and to abstain from evil and immorality.

When it came to giving content to these general exhortations, Paul and his converts did not always see eye to eye. There were two reasons for this. He was, firstly, a *Jewish* apostle to *Gentiles*, many or most of whom had been idolaters and had participated fully in the common Graeco-Roman society. His inbred views of behaviour he regarded as obviously correct, and this is what sometimes led to conflict with his Gentile converts. He mostly responded by admonition and rebuke, only occasionally being pushed to think through an issue afresh, on the basis of his new Christian principles.

The second source of conflict over behaviour was that the members of his churches sometimes thought through the practical consequences of Paul's own theology in a way different from his. These two sources of disagreement often overlapped. He thought that his followers should imitate him, and he viewed his own behaviour as resulting from the Spirit of God which dwelt within him. Since his converts had that same Spirit, he thought that their behaviour should be like his; and his behaviour was, on the whole, Jewish. He might debate with others on Christian theological grounds, but the outside observer can often tell that the real difference was between Jewish and Gentile assumptions.

Paul's most famous chapter was written because he and the Corinthians thought through his own principles in different ways. He had told them, as he told everyone, to love one another and to live by the Spirit. After he left, reports from Corinth led him to think that they were living by the Spirit in an exaggerated and unfortunate way, but not loving one another well enough. They emphasized a charismatic gift, speaking in 'tongues', a gift which Paul also had—more than any of them, by his own admission (1 Cor. 14: 18). He spends three chapters on the topic, almost as many as on the law. He urges that tongues are not an especially valuable spiritual gift; in fact, speaking in tongues is the lowest on his list (1 Cor. 12: 28–31; 14: 1–5). He tries to bring them down to earth: 'since you are eager for manifestations of the Spirit, strive to excel in building up the church' (14: 12); 'in church I would rather speak five words with my mind, in order to instruct others, than ten thousand words in a tongue' (14: 19).

The Corinthians fell short with respect to love of one another, as his discussion of their assemblies indicates. There were factions. Further, they did not share the Lord's supper equally, but rather brought their own food, with the result that some had more than others (11: 17–22).

Paul rose to the occasion by writing 1 Corinthians 13. If he had written nothing else, his fame would be deserved. It begins as a rebuke to those who pride themselves because they babble when possessed by the Spirit: 'If I speak in the tongues of men and of angels, but have not love, I am a noisy gong or a clanging cymbal.' He proceeds to explain what it is about love which makes it the greatest of all gifts of the Spirit:

Love is patient and kind; love is not jealous or boastful; it is not arrogant or rude. Love does not insist on its own way; it is not irritable or resentful; it does not rejoice at wrong, but rejoices in the right. Love bears all things, believes all things, hopes all things, endures all things. (13: 4–7)

The other spiritual gifts, such as tongues and prophecy, will cease, but love will not. 'So faith, hope, love abide, these three; but the greatest of these is love' (13: 13).

These three chapters show Paul at his pastoral best, partly because he is so obviously right. The mode of argument is revealing. It does not twist and turn, it is not tortuous. The law gave him a problem; the relative importance of love and charismatic displays did not.

Other questions of behaviour fall somewhere in between. We shall turn to the most instructive point for gaining an overall appreciation of Paul and his circumstances: a Jewish apostle seeking to win Gentiles, who formally said that they were not bound by the law, but who generally thought that they should do what it says. On many points Jewish and Gentile standards of behaviour were the same. No one favoured murder, theft, robbery, deceit and the like, and when Paul lists good and bad behaviour (see just below) many pagan parallels to most of the items in his lists can be brought forward. There were two great issues on which Jews and Gentiles disagreed: idolatry and some aspects of sexual behaviour. Jewish criticisms of Gentiles usually focused on these two points (for example, Wisdom of Solomon 13–14). They dominate Paul's 'vice lists', the passages where he gives a whole string of sins. In Romans 1 the attack on Gentiles proceeds from idolatry to sexual immorality, both of which are treated in some detail (1: 19–27). Only then are other sins introduced, which are listed rather than discussed (1: 28–31). In 1 Corinthians 5: 11 the first item in the list is sexual immorality (*porneia*, misleadingly translated simply as 'immorality' by the RSV), and the third is idolatry. In 1 Corinthians 6: 9f. the first item is sexual immorality and the second is idolatry; specific kinds of sexual immorality then follow (adultery and homosexuality). In Galatians 5: 19–21 the list is headed by sexual immorality, impurity, licentiousness, and idolatry. These lists all show the influence of the Diaspora synagogue.

We have already discussed the principal topic which brought Christians into contact with idolatry: eating food which had been offered to an idol (pp. 88–90). In order to see the degree to which Paul's presuppositions about behaviour were Jewish, and the way in which these assumptions brought him into conflict with his Gentile converts, we can best focus now on the second topic, sex. I do not want to give the false impression that sex was the point which was most important to Paul. This is, in any case, a risk that will be run.

We shall, however, be on the lookout for the other source of conflict: the interpretation of Paul's own theological principles, which were potentially more revolutionary than he himself, a social conservative, realized. Most of the problems arise in I Corinthians, and we shall take them in the order in which they occur.

Sexual behaviour

Incest: One of Paul's converts was living with 'his father's wife', probably his stepmother (see Deut. 22: 30; 27: 20; Lev. 18: 8). Paul correctly says that this kind of sexual immorality 'is not found even among pagans' (1 Cor. 5: 1). He brands this as a type of *porneia*, a word which he and others used as a general term to cover all forms of sexual transgression. Paul prescribes that the man be expelled from the church, being 'delivered to Satan for the destruction of the flesh' (1 Cor. 5: 4–5). It appears from this that he thought that the man would be punished by death, not at the hands of humans, but simply by being turned over to Satan. He adds, however, that 'his spirit will be saved in the day of the Lord Jesus' (5: 5).

This is a most instructive clash. Here the transgressor was not following standard Gentile mores. He seems to have thought that his deed was justified by his new Christian status. The sentence in 1 Corinthians 5: 3–4 is quite difficult, but the most likely rendering of it is this:

For I, though absent in body, am present in the Spirit, [and] I have already condemned, as though present, the one who is acting thus in the name of the Lord Jesus. When you are gathered together ... hand this man over to Satan.

Most translators, seeking to avoid the implication that the man committed incest 'in the name of the Lord Jesus', connect that phrase either with 'I have condemned' or 'when you are gathered together'. The simplest rendering, however, is that given just above, and this also provides the readiest explanation of the man's behaviour: he acted 'in the name of the Lord Jesus'. It is clear what had happened: Paul had said 'you are a new creation' and 'live in the Spirit'. The man took seriously his being a new person and concluded that old relationships had passed away. He then consulted the spirit within him and began cohabiting with his stepmother. He had thought through Paul's own principles in a way Paul had not considered, and he accepted a revolutionary implication of Paul's theology which offended Paul himself.

We see also how loath Paul was to condemn a member of the body of Christ to eternal destruction. He avoided it by accepting the Jewish principle that physical death atones for sins, and he maintained that the destruction of the body would lead to the salvation of the spirit.

Marriage and celibacy: In replying to a question from the Corinthians about marriage and celibacy, Paul several times indicated that he preferred the latter: it was 'good for a man not to touch a woman' (1 Cor. 7: 1); he himself was celibate and did not travel with a wife as did other apostles (1 Cor. 9: 5), and he wished that all were as he (7: 7). His preference was repeated in 7: 28, 32–5, and 7: 38. A widow would in his judgement do better to remain a widow that to remarry (7: 40).

Paul based his advice on two points. One was that married partners are concerned more about each other than about 'the affairs of the Lord', 'how to be holy in body and spirit' (7: 32–4). The other was that marriage is commitment to a world which was rapidly passing away (7: 29, 31). In view of the shortness of time people should not change. This applied to being married or single, slave or free, circumcised or uncircumcised (7: 17–24). Thus Paul based his preference for celibacy on new, Christian principles, the nearness of the end and the work of the Lord, but the net result was extremely conservative: do not change.

Paul's preference for asceticism, however, may have been natural to him and very probably preceded his call to be an apostle. We cannot suppose that, when called, he either divorced or left his wife at home. Either action would have violated his own rules about marriage (see just below). Before his call he was probably already a full-time zealot, with no time for marriage. Then the principles would have been different, but the result the same. To some degree Paul's own behaviour may have been based on Cynic 'role-models'. Many of these wandering preachers could have said of themselves what Paul said: they taught 'in hunger and thirst . . . ill-clad and buffeted and homeless' (1 Cor. 4: 11), and in these circumstances they were naturally without wives.

Thus Paul's preference for asceticism may have been purely personal. He was ascetic; he was an apostle; apostles should be imitated; therefore Christians should seriously consider asceticism. Yet we must say to his credit that he did not try to force it on his congregations. He reckoned with sexual desire as natural, and he allowed for it. Within marriage, partners should 'rule over' each other's bodies, the man over the woman's, but also the woman over the man's. Though they might refrain from sex for a while in order to devote themselves to prayer, they should satisfy each other sexually (7: 3–5). Young people, not yet married, would be better advised to marry than to commit sexual transgression, and the same rule applied to widows (7: 8–9; 36–40). As often as Paul repeats his preference for celibacy, so often also does he say that marriage is proper and that sex within it is right.

Remarriage as adultery: Paul regarded it as adultery for a divorced person to remarry if the spouse was still alive. Here he offers one of his rare quotations of material attributed to Jesus:

To the married I give charge, not I but the Lord, that the wife should not separate from her husband (but if she does, let her remain single or else be reconciled to her husband)—and that the husband should not divorce his wife. (1 Cor. 7: 10–11)

One version of the saying of Jesus as it is found in the synoptic gospels prohibits divorce entirely (Mark 10: 2–9; Matt. 19: 3–9), while another prohibits only remarriage while the first partner is still alive (Matt. 5: 31–2; Luke 16: 18). Paul knew the second tradition, as is clear from the saying just quoted, and also from 1 Corinthians 7: 39 (cf. Rom. 7: 1–3). This is a stricter view than was common in Judaism, but the prohibition of remarriage to another partner is also known from the *Covenant of Damascus*, one of the Dead Sea Scrolls.

Prostitution: We here come to a point which reveals the existence of views about sex in Diaspora Judaism which were stricter than would be expected on the basis of the Bible and most Palestinian material. In 1 Corinthians 6: 13b–20 Paul condemns, as *porneia*, the use of a prostitute. He brings heavy artillery to bear: the body of the Christian is part of the body of Christ. 'Will you', he asks, 'take the members of Christ and make them members of a prostitute?' He has a second argument: 'your body is a temple of the Holy Spirit within you, which you have from God', and therefore one should not defile the temple with the impurity of *porneia*.

It is possible that Paul first conceived the notion of union with Christ and then considered all the other unions which were inappropriate to it and which might damage it. We should be prepared, however, to distinguish rationale from motive and source. It is also possible that he first thought that the employment of a prostitute was wrong and then went in search of an argument to prove it. The argument, of course, is interesting, since it is another illustration of the fact that Paul based ethical injunctions on the idea of participation in Christ, not on a supposed doctrine of legal justification. But it is likely that the argument about union with Christ and being the temple of the Spirit is rationalization to support a point arrived at on another basis: he was Jewish and followed strict Diaspora practice.

Judaism, one would have thought in advance, did not condemn prostitution. The profession is accepted (though not applauded) in the Bible, and the Rabbis subsequently considered it legal. Rahab, a Canaanite prostitute, was a heroine (Joshua 2). Josephus, summarizing common Judaism, wrote that the wages of a prostitute could not be used to purchase a sacrifice (*Antiquities* 4: 206; cf. 4: 245). It follows from this that prostitution was not considered completely wrong. But in the Diaspora, and perhaps also in Palestine, there was a more rigorous view.

We find it in Philo: according to *Special Laws* 3: 51 the law of Moses requires that a harlot (*pornē*) be stoned. *On Joseph* 43 is even stronger: 'Other nations are permitted after the fourteenth year to deal ... with harlots [*pornai*] ... but with us a courtesan [*hetaira*] is not even permitted to live.' A courtesan in the Greek world was socially acceptable, at least on some occasions. Unlike a common prostitute, who was considered unfit for society, or a wife, who was sequestered from it, a courtesan could attend with her lover the symposia, meetings for discussion and drinking. Thus Philo's view goes against common Graeco-Roman culture. Further, it goes beyond the law of Moses, which does not prescribe death for a prostitute. If Philo had a text in mind it was probably Deuteronomy 23: 17, which in the Greek translation (23: 18 in the Septuagint) prohibits a daughter of Israel from being a prostitute. But still his view was stricter than the Bible.

It is likely that in the Diaspora, faced with *porneia* of all kinds, some Jews attempted to forbid prostitution entirely within their own communities (a step which was not required in Palestine, where the problem of Gentile sexual ethics did not press so heavily), and that the Septuagint and Philo show two different but related efforts in this direction. Some such influence as this is, I propose, behind the extremely strong argument of Paul against the use of a prostitute.

Homosexual activity: Paul was against homosexuality, both active and inactive, both male and female. This marks him as Jewish. Since homosexuality in the Graeco-Roman world is not widely understood, I shall first lay out the issue.

There was no condemnation of sexual relations with a person of the same sex simply because of the sameness. Far from homosexual attraction and activity being condemned, in some circles they were positively valued as part of educational and cultural life. In classical Athens, for example, it was thought that a boy or youth should be honourably courted by a man, who should desire to lead him into wisdom and bravery. The man was also expected to desire the boy sexually. The young male body was generally regarded as the greatest beauty in nature, and therefore as highly desirable. If the man was worthy, he inspired in the boy not *eros*, sexual desire, but *philos*, love without lust. The boy, motivated by *philos*, might grant the man's desire, but preferably intercourse took place only between the thighs, with no penetration. Further, the taboo held that the boy should not himself enjoy the physical aspect.

How often this chaste ideal was met we cannot know, and certainly there were many abuses, which were themselves condemned by pagans. But we note, first, that homosexuality of this sort was, at least sometimes, idealized and favourably evaluated. Even in Rome, where this particular aesthetic theory did not hold sway, it was regarded as normal for an adult male to desire boys. Homosexual activity, like any form of sex, was sometimes satirized, and some seductions were even against the law, but nevertheless there was no general condemnation. This sets Graeco-Roman culture off sharply from Jewish culture.

Secondly, we note the reservation about penetration. The general view was that it was shameful for a male to be the passive partner. Even if a boy granted his adult lover the full favour in his youth, he should grow up to take the active role. In classical Athens, for an adult male to be passive was a bar to the exercise of citizenship. Slaves could serve as passive partners, and of course so could women. The Greeks and Romans despised effeminacy in men. It seems that the strength of this taboo weakened in the later Roman period, but it was strong enough in the first century for there to be ridicule of even Julius Caesar for playing the passive role. When Curio quipped that Caesar was 'every woman's husband and every man's wife', the ridicule was in part directed at his general promiscuity, but the real bite comes in the second half: with men Caesar took the woman's role. One more example: Seneca ridiculed a wealthy man because he kept a handsome slave who was dressed like a woman when he waited at table, but became the man in private. What drew comment was that the master rather than the slave played the passive role in sex.

It is a curiosity of human behaviour that the active partner, though he may have disgraced his passive lover—making him like a slave or woman—shared none of the blame. (Modern society is equally hypocritical about prostitution.) In the Graeco-

Roman world men were expected to be sexually active, and they had little to fear from public opinion, or from the malice of friends and confidants, if they engaged in homosexual activity on the giving rather than the receiving end.

We have much less information about female homosexuality. We hear of one woman who shaved her head and who bragged about how many women she could have each day. Her behaviour was not applauded, probably because of her aggressive assumption of the male role.

Jews, looking at the Gentile world, saw it as full of *porneia*, sexual sin of all sorts, and homosexuality was a prime case. They condemned it lock, stock, and barrel. This is emphasized in the Bible (for example, Lev. 18: 22) and repeated in subsequent Jewish literature. In the *Letter of Aristeas* (written by an Egyptian Jew in the second century BCE) we read that most non-Jewish men defile themselves by homosexual intercourse and that 'whole countries and cities pride themselves upon such vices' (*Letter of Aristeas* 152 f.). The Jewish *Sibylline Oracle* 2: 73 contains the prohibition *mē arsenokoitein*, literally 'do not bugger males', putting the activity on a par with extortion and murder. We note that it is the active role which is condemned. Philo, in a substantial discussion of sexual sins, lists homosexuality as next to bestiality in gravity. Making love to boys, pederasty (*to paiderastein*), is common in Gentile society, and Philo especially complains that men boast not only of the active but also of the passive role. There then follows a full description of the wiles and seductive manner of passive males. He points out that the law, that is, Moses' law, provides death as the penalty for the male who dresses like a woman; he adds, 'the lover of such (*ho paiderastēs*) may be assured that he is subject to the same penalty' (*Special Laws* 3: 37–42). Again, there is condemnation even of the active male.

So, when we turn to Paul, we are not surprised that he condemns all homosexual activity, nor that he specifies both the active and the passive partners. Out of an excess of modesty some English translations do not precisely render 1 Corinthians 6: 9. The RSV has 'sexual perverts' and the NEB 'homosexual perversion'. The Jerusalem Bible correctly has 'catamites' and 'sodomites'. Paul names both the effeminate partner, the *mala-kos*, 'soft' one, and the active one, the *arsenokoitēs*. Some scholars propose that the words are uncertain as to meaning and thus that perhaps Paul did not really condemn homosexuality. The words, however, are quite clear. 'Soft' was a common term for the passive partner, and nothing could be more explicit than 'one who buggers males'. We noted the word in the *Sibylline Oracle* 2: 73, and both that passage and Paul's reflect the ter-minology of Leviticus 18: 22 and 20: 13: *meta arsenos koitēn*, 'he who has coitus with a male'. In another passage, Romans 1: 26–7, Paul condemns both male and female homosexuality in blanket terms and without making any distinctions.

With regard to the source of these passages: Romans 1: 18–32 is very close to the Wisdom of Solomon, a Jewish book written in Egypt. Further, Paul's reference to 'images resembling mortal man or birds or animals or reptiles' (Rom. 1: 23) points to an origin in the synagogues of Egypt. (Birds, animals and reptiles were idolized in Egypt, not commonly in the rest of the Graeco-Roman world.) 1 Corinthians 6: 9–10 is pre-Pauline in origin. The language of the unrighteous not inheriting the kingdom of God and the list of sins which follows point to a traditional Jewish formulation, one perhaps passed on to Paul by the Jewish-Christian community before him, but possibly simply remembered from synagogue sermons. In short, the two con-demnations of homosexuality show that he applied to his Gen-tile converts the standards of Judaism. Naturally he found them wanting: 'such were some of you' (1 Cor. 6: 11). We see here a conflict between the Jewish apostle and his Gentile followers.

Desire and marriage: For our last case we leave Corinth and go to Thessalonica. While there, Paul had told the Thessalonians to avoid *porneia* (1 Thess. 4: 2). When he wrote to them a little later, he specified one type in particular. Each male should know how to 'take his own vessel in holiness and honour', not 'with the feeling of desire' as 'the Gentiles' do. 'Vessel' is evidently a metaphor for 'wife': the vessel is something which a male can 'take' in the right way, avoiding *porneia*. It must be the wife, since there is no other 'vessel' which can be used sexually but still 'in holiness and honour'. The verb translated 'take' is more literally 'get' or 'acquire', and thus the admonition may be that one should not 'acquire' a wife for the purpose of fulfilling passionate desire.

We saw above that Paul recognized physical desire and did not think that he could legislate it out of existence. Further, elementary facts of life indicate that a certain amount of desire is necessary for the sex act to take place at all. Since he did not forbid sexual relations, he could not attempt completely to eliminate desire. He wished, rather, to limit it to a subordinate place, or possibly to encourage his converts to marry for other reasons. Marriage may satisfy desire, but it should not be undertaken simply because of it. 1 Corinthians 7, where marriage for the sake of desire is recognized, and 1 Thessalonians, where desire is to be restricted, were written some years apart, and Paul could have changed his mind. The admonition in 1 Thessalonians, however, is not truly a contradiction to the advice at the end of 1 Corinthians 7 that unmarried couples should marry if they cannot control their passions. He could have said in the same breath 'do not marry simply because of physical desire' and 'if physical desire is overwhelming, it is better to marry'.

Where did Paul get the wish to limit the role of desire in marriage? The passage in 1 Thessalonians is thoroughly Jewish. He tells the Thessalonians, who were Gentiles (see 1: 9), not to act like Gentiles (4: 5, RSV 'heathen'); that is, Paul writes to them as if they were Jewish, and he probably simply borrowed a standard synagogal homily. Thus the view that passionate desire should not be the dominant consideration in marriage is probably Jewish.

But where did Judaism get it, and what form of Judaism was it? One stream of Greek thought was anti-passion. Socrates, and apparently Plato as well, was in favour of reducing 'to an unavoidable minimum all activity of which the end is physical enjoyment, in order that the irrational and appetitive element of the soul may not be encouraged and strengthened by indulgence' (J. K. Dover). Some Stoics, such as Musonius Rufus, also held that sexual relations should serve only the purpose of procreation. This view was picked up by Philo and was held by him to be a principle of Jewish life. He said that Jewish males as well as females married as virgins, and that even within marriage desire should not be the reason for intercourse: 'The end we seek in wedlock is not pleasure [*hēdonē*], but the begetting of lawful children' (*On Joseph* 43). We find the same point in one of Josephus's summaries of the Jewish law: 'The Law recognizes no sexual connexions, except the natural union of man and wife, and that only for the procreation of children' (*Against Apion* 2: 199).

It seems, then, that 1 Thessalonians 4: 3–8 is more Jewish ethical material, coming from a strict and partially ascetic stream of Diaspora Judaism.

Conclusion

In Paul's discussions of sex there are two types of material in terms of form, vice lists (and related material), and substantial discussions. Many of Paul's references to sex are in vice lists and the allied homiletical discussion of Romans 1: 18–32. The vice lists are traditional Jewish homiletical material: they emphasize the two cardinal Gentile errors as seen by Jews: idolatry and sexual transgression. In some cases, Paul's views are closely related to those of Jewish thinkers who were influenced by partially ascetic and pleasure-denying forms of pagan philosophy. When he is passing on this traditional material, especially when he does so in lists, he seems inflexible and unsympathetic:

Do not be deceived; neither the sexually immoral, nor idolaters, nor adulterers, nor catamites, nor sodomites, nor thieves, nor the greedy, nor drunkards, nor revilers, nor robbers will inherit the kingdom of God. (1 Cor. 6: 9f.)

Whole masses of people are thus consigned to perdition in sweeping terms.

Only when circumstances forced him to leave his traditional lists do we meet his characteristic virtuosity, and we also find a good deal more sympathy. One of his converts was actually living in an incestuous relationship, perhaps justifying his doing so on the grounds of Paul's own preaching of the new creation.

Here we find fresh thinking. Paul does not follow the traditional practice of roundly condemning transgressors to destruction, but proposes that the man's soul would be saved. Conceivably, had one of his own parishioners engaged in homosexual activity, Paul would have re-thought that issue too. When forced to think, he was a creative theologian; but on ethical issues he was seldom forced to think, and simply sought to impose Jewish behaviour on his Gentile converts.

This was the case with regard to topics other than sex. When, however, his converts argued with him on the basis of Christian principles which he had taught them, as the Corinthians did on the question of food offered to idols, he was capable of reconsidering the issue and modifying his opinions. When his own message of living in the Spirit led to excessive charismatic displays, he countered with a precise analysis of what was wrong with such behaviour and a moving description of the love which should characterize Christians. He offers, therefore, the beginnings of a code of behaviour that is founded on the Jewish principle of love of neighbour and his new principle of union with Christ.

11 The salvation of Israel and of the world: Romans 9–11

The dilemma

We return now to Paul's fundamental theological problem: how to hold together the two dispensations, one being God's election of Israel and his gift to them of the law, the other his offer of salvation to all who have faith in Christ. The election of Israel posed an even harder problem than did the law. In the introductory verses of Romans 9 Paul itemizes the signs of God's favour, but he also grieves:

I have great sorrow and unceasing anguish in my heart. For I could wish that I myself were accursed and cut off from Christ for the sake of my brethren, my kin by race. They are Israelites, and to them belong the sonship, the glory, the covenants, the giving of the law, the [temple] worship and the promises. (Rom. 9: 2–4)

Why such grief? why the wish that he could be 'cut off' for their sake? Obviously he thinks that most Israelites have themselves been cut off. We noted briefly in discussing 'righteoused by faith' that Paul required faith in Christ not only of Gentiles but also of Jews. He and Peter, good Jews, were righteoused only by faith (Gal. 2: 15). God had determined to righteous both the uncircumcised and the circumcised by faith (Rom. 3: 30). In Romans 11 he uses the image of an olive tree. Many of the native branches have been lopped off. They can be grafted back in only on the basis of faith (11: 17–24, especially verse 23). Faith is not the general attitude of trusting God, but the specific commitment to Christ. Though he uses Abraham, who could not have known about Jesus, as the biblical paradigm of the faithful person, Paul thought that in his own time faith was Christian faith. 'Now that faith has come' (Gal. 3: 25) refers to the coming of Christ, and the faith that he and Peter shared was in Christ.

The fact that most Jews did not have this faith caused an 'existential' problem: he was worried about the fate of other individual human beings, in this case his 'kin by race'.

But he also had a theological problem in the strict sense of the word: the problem of God's constancy. We have seen throughout our study how Paul insisted on God's unchanging will. His hardest problem with regard to the law was God's intention in giving it. The election of Israel, however, called God's consistency of purpose even more into question: why choose Israel, give them the law, and then require them to be saved as were Gentiles—by faith in Christ? Doubts about God's constancy led to the theological problem called 'theodicy', the 'righteousness of God'. God, we have seen, should not be capricious. And so the lead question is whether or not the word of God, when he called Israel, had failed (Rom. 9: 6). Has God been fair, honest, just, reliable, and constant? The two dispensations seem to indicate not. Only if Paul can hold them together can he save God's reputation.

Romans 9–11 begins with these two questions, the fate of Jews and God's fairness, and they lead on to a third: the fate of the universe. The context in which these questions were raised is important. Paul had finished his work in Asia Minor and Greece, and he wanted to press on to Spain; first the offering of the Gentiles had to be taken to Jerusalem. The 'completion' of Paul's own work (as he thought of it) meant that the Lord would soon return, and so he had to press the question of God's overall plan. If the plan was to save first the Jew and then the Greek (Rom. 1: 16; 2: 9) something was amiss. Paul's Gentiles were ready, but Peter's mission to the Jews had been less successful. Thus the anguish of the opening verses: Paul's kin by race might not accept the Lord when he returned; they would be lost, and this would also mean that God's election of Israel was of no effect.

In Romans 9–11 one finds seven major assertions: (1) Despite appearances, God is just; (2) Israel was elect and remains so; (3) The election was always selective and never covered every descendant of Abraham; (4) Israel, at least at present, has 'stumbled'; (5) God will save only those who have faith in Christ; (6)

All Israel will be saved; (7) Everyone and everything will be saved.

Our chapter can by no means do justice to Paul's three chapters, written with so much anguish, hope, and faith. These partially contradictory assertions ebb and flow in the chapters as Paul seeks solid ground. On the question of God's justice, he has little to say, and one is almost embarrassed on his behalf. He proposes that the pot may not criticize the potter, and that similarly humans may not object to God, who predestines some to salvation but rejects others. This and other attempts in Romans 9–11 to deal directly with the problem of theodicy are standard in Jewish literature, and they show none of Paul's customary virtuosity and ingenuity.

In this discussion we shall focus on a few main questions: (1) In the passages which indicate that not all Israel is in the people of God, what is the reasoning? That is, what is Israel's fault? (2) What is Paul's solution to his dilemma that God chose Israel and has not wavered on the point ('the gifts and the call of God are irrevocable', in 11: 29), but that nevertheless he saves through Christ? (3) Does the view that Israel will be saved presuppose that all Israelites will come to have faith in Christ? (4) What shall we make of the assertion of universal salvation?

Israel's fault

First of all, Paul attributes the non-inclusion of part of Israel to God's predestination (Rom. 9: 6–29). God has 'hardened' them (11: 25). But we have seen repeatedly that God's providence or predestination does not mean that humans are not responsible. Thus we must ask what, from Israel's point of view, was wrong.

The first and most obvious answer is that most Israelites do not have faith in Jesus Christ. That is the main point of Romans 9: 30–2 (the stumbling stone is Christ); 10: 9–13; 10: 14–17 (which backs up 10: 13); and, most important, the passage on the olive tree, 11: 17–24. We note especially 11: 23: 'Even the others, if they do not persist in their lack of faith, will be grafted in.'

In addition to lack of faith in Christ, is anything else wrong?

Traditional Protestant scholarship holds that Paul accuses his kin by race of self-righteousness. There are three verses which have been taken in this way:

> 9: 32: They pursued 'it' (righteousness or law) as though it were based on works
>
> 10: 3: they sought to establish their own righteousness
>
> 11: 6: 'it' (election) is by grace, not on the basis of works

The precise meaning of Romans 9: 32 cannot be determined. Verses 31–2, literally translated, say this: 'But Israel, pursuing a law of righteousness, did not reach law. Why? Because [they pursued it] not on the basis of faith but as [if it were] on the basis of works.' The meaning of 'did not reach law' is obscure, and one cannot base much on the phrase. Many suppose that 'as on the basis of works' means, 'Each and every Jew thought that righteousness could be earned by effort. They all made the effort, thought they had succeeded, and thus became self-righteous. They are rightly condemned.' The first problem with this view is that it would condemn Paul, his fellow workers and followers, all of whom made strenuous efforts to be blameless, or at least were urged to do so by him. Secondly, this construal is anachronistic. In this section Paul is not thinking in this individualizing and psychologizing way. He did not fix on a general failing, self-righteousness, and accuse all living Jews of it. He contrasted two dispensations, 'faith' and 'the law', and accused Israel of choosing the wrong one. In dealing with the fate of his kin by race, he was not worried about the self-righteousness of some individuals, but about the Jews as a whole and God's promise to the people of Israel. Romans 9: 31–2, however, will never reveal much; the sentence is obscure, and Paul's meaning must be inferred from what follows, about which there is no doubt.

Israel stumbled on the stone of stumbling (Rom. 9: 32–3), which he takes to be Christ. In the proof text of 9: 33 we find 'the person who has faith in *it* will not be put to shame', which Paul almost certainly took to mean 'in *him*', Christ. ('Stone', *lithos*, is masculine. The contrast between 'it' and 'him' is a contrast only in English, not in Greek.) Thus in 9: 33 Israel's fault is not having faith in Christ.

Romans 10: 3 is commonly understood to be a clear accusation of self-righteousness. 'They sought to establish their own righteousness' is taken to mean 'each Jew individually tried to earn God's favour by meritorious achievement'. Some scholars, noting that 'zeal' appears in 10: 2, propose that this describes the fault of Israel. One wrote that 'zeal for the law can altogether alienate man from God, and has precisely the effect of making him a sinner'. Paul, however, did not agree with this view of zeal. He thought that it was a good thing, and he praises Jews for it: 'I testify on their behalf that they have zeal for God.' Unfortunately, it is 'not according to knowledge' (10: 2). They do not recognize Christ, and so they aim at the wrong goal. 'Being ignorant of God's righteousness, and trying to establish their own, they did not obey the righteousness of God' (10: 3). They erred by seeking the wrong righteousness, not by the act of seeking.

How is the right goal defined? 'God's righteousness', which is contrasted to 'their own', is for '*all* who *have faith*': it is available to Jew and Gentile equally on the basis of faith in Christ. This brings to an end the other righteousness, by law (Rom. 10: 4). 'Their own righteousness' is the righteousness peculiar to Jews as a group, not that earned by individuals. Jewish righteousness springs from loyalty to the law of Moses, which applies only to Jews, and which is thus 'their own' and is not 'for all'. Paul's focus in Romans 10: 1–4 is, again, historical and communal: he is thinking of the people of Israel as a group and the relation of the Mosaic dispensation to God's plan of salvation. He is not analysing the interior effect of the law on the individual Jew. The people of Israel posed a problem because, on the whole, they persisted in accepting the first dispensation and did not see that God had offered another.

We pause here to note the significance of our passage for understanding the word 'righteousness'. In Galatians and the rest of Romans, Paul argued that righteousness is not by the law but by faith—or, more accurately translating his verbal formulation, 'one is righteoused by faith not by law'. Up to this point, he has written about only one righteousness and has debated how it is attained: by obedience to Christ or to the law. In

Romans 10, however, he distinguishes between two righteous-nesses, Jewish righteousness, which is by the law, and God's righteousness, which is by faith. That is also the formulation of Philippians 3: 6 and 3: 9; 'righteousness by the law', which Paul as an obedient Jew once had, is contrasted to 'righteousness based on faith in Christ'. The truth finally comes out: there is such a thing as righteousness by the law. Further, it is not wicked. In and of itself it is 'gain' (Phil. 3: 9). It becomes wrong only because God has revealed another one.

Paul's accusation in the final verses of Romans 9 and the first four verses of Romans 10, which we see even more clearly when we compare Philippians 3: 2–11, is that the fault of Jewish righteousness is its exclusivity. God had called Israel to be a people apart, and they had obeyed. The present generation of Jews do not perceive that Christ has brought an end to that epoch. God, Paul thought, does not want them to remain sep-arate. It is poignant to note that Paul himself had not entirely surrendered the view that Jews have priority in God's plan (see Rom. 3: 1–4; 9: 4–6). They are so important that even rejecting them means 'the reconciliation of the world' (11: 15).

Romans 11: 6 ('if it is by grace, it is no longer on the basis of works') is the only passage in the extant letters which puts the contrast between two abstractions, grace and works. I note both the contrast and also that it is unusual. This formulation is probably short for 'by God's grace bestowed on those who have faith in Christ, not by obedience to the Mosaic law'. This verse should not lead us to think that Paul primarily thought in terms of individualized and generalized abstractions. The problem in these chapters is the concrete one of Israel's refusal to accept the grace of God as recently revealed, not the individual's effort or lack of it. The Jews have one fault, but only one: rejecting Jesus as the Christ.

Paul's solution to his dilemma

We recall the dilemma: reconciling God's promises to Israel with the promise of salvation to those who have faith in Christ. He offers a solution repeatedly in Romans 11. Salvation, he proposes, has come to the Gentiles first, 'so as to make Israel jealous'. This is directly connected with Paul's own work: he 'glorifies' his ministry, 'so that I may make my kin jealous, and I will save some of them' (11: 11–14). The clue is 'make jealous'. God will save Israel by means of the Gentile mission, which will make them jealous and lead them to accept Christ. One of Paul's problems had been that his Gentiles were ready but the Jews were not. How could this be, since the plan was 'to the Jew first, then to the Greek'? He now proposes that the plan of salvation has been reversed and that the Gentiles will enter the people of God first. For the first time Paul assigns himself responsibility for the salvation of Israel—but only indirect responsibility. He modestly says, to be sure, 'I will save some of them'. But, since the Jerusalem apostles had not done very well, he thinks that it is now up to him, and God will make use even of his boasting.

Paul repeats the change of sequence twice more. According to Romans 11: 25–7, Israel has been temporarily hardened (by God), but hardened only until 'the full number of the Gentiles come in', and *thus* (that is, by means of the entry of Gentiles) 'all Israel will be saved'. This great reversal of the divine plan is taken to its logical conclusion in 11: 30–1: Israel's present disobedience makes the mercy of God shift to the Gentiles, but the inclusion of Gentiles will result in the salvation of Israel: and finally all people will be saved (11: 32).

God is still in charge, and the disobedience of the Jews, which is ultimately in his hands, is for a purpose. It has allowed time for the mission to the Gentiles. The Jewish rejection of the gospel, their disobedience, has been the agency by which the Gentiles received it. Now that Gentiles—or at least their full number—are, or soon will be, in the people of God, God will direct his mercy through the Gentiles back to the Jews, using jealousy to accomplish his purpose.

Now at last we see the Paul whom we have come to know and either love or marvel at. It is an ingenious revision of the plan of salvation, and in the revised plan everything works for the good, even disobedience. As with the law, which 'made sin sinful', so with the rejection of the gospel by Israel. It is part of God's will, and in the end he will use disobedience for his own purpose; and all will be saved.

Is the prediction of salvation for Israel dependent on *all the individuals in Israel* coming to have faith in Christ? We can divide this question into two sub-questions: Does 'all Israel' in Romans 11: 26 mean 'every Israelite'? Does Paul promise salvation to 'all Israel' apart from faith in Christ?

There are two possible understandings of 'all Israel': 'every Israelite' and 'the full and proper representation of Israel'. Let us lay out the relevant phrases, starting with what is said about Gentiles. We know that Paul did not think that he had succeeded in winning every Gentile, and thus when in 11: 25 we meet the phrase 'the fullness' or 'completeness' of the Gentiles, we are prepared to take this as do the RSV and most commentators: the full number of the Gentiles, that is, not all, just those who were (from God's point of view) chosen and who (on their side) responded to the call with faith. Earlier in Romans 11 are two phrases about the Jews. In the first Paul contrasts 'their rejection' with 'their completeness' (11: 12). Since the contrast is sweeping, the natural inclination is to think of 'complete inclusion'. In 11: 14, however, Paul says that he will 'save some of them'. Does this mean that only some will be saved, or that Paul will not himself manage to do all the saving? The image of the olive tree, which follows, clearly points towards the meaning 'some will be saved'. Verse 23 seems decisive: the others will be grafted back in 'if they do not remain faithless'. Faith is the condition of inclusion, and Paul excludes those who do not have it. All in all, then, at the end of the olive tree passage we are ready to think that Paul really meant 'some will be saved' in 11: 14, and that 'their completeness' in 11: 12 is the same as the 'completeness' of the Gentiles in 11: 25: the full and correct number, as God has determined it.

We are, then, a bit surprised at 'all' in 11: 26, 'and thus [by the reversed sequence] all Israel will be saved'. Has Paul changed his mind? Will Israel be given an advantage after all? Will God save them even if they do not begin to have faith in Jesus as Christ?

Some scholars think so. They can point to the proof text of

Romans 11: 26 f., which says that the Redeemer will come and remove iniquity from Jacob; that is, from the people of Israel as defined by physical descent. Paul, in this view, accepts covenantal theology: God has made a covenant with Israel, and he will keep it, whether they are obedient or not. Having rejected physical descent as the basis of salvation in chapter 9, Paul now accepts it.

But does Romans 11: 25–7 reverse the view of 11: 17–24 (the olive tree)? From 9: 1 through to 11: 24 the point is that, no matter how many or how few get saved, it will be only through faith in Jesus Christ. Does 'all Israel' in verse 26 retract that? Does Paul, after all, favour Israel?

'All Israel' (Rom. 11: 26) is not actually in contradiction to 'as many as have faith' (11: 23), because the topic changes. If the subject is ordinary history, in which apostles and others proclaim faith, and people either respond or not, Paul will uniformly answer: those who accept with faith are in, those who do not are out. But we note that the proof text in 11: 26b–7 shifts the ground. It does not apply to the period during which the apostles preach the gospel, but to the time when the Redeemer comes from Zion. Not only does the ground shift when the proof text is quoted, it remains shifted. The passage goes on to promise salvation ('mercy') to *all people* (11: 32). In 11: 25 or 26 Paul moves from 'what happens to those Israelites who reject the gospel while Peter and I are preaching it?' to another and grander theme: God will ultimately save everybody. Not only that, he will save everything. 'From him and through him and unto him are *ta panta*, all things' (11: 36).

This is a triumph of what is now called lateral thinking. Paul has already solved one knotty problem (his Gentiles being ready before Peter's Jews) but he still has the hardest one before him: why did God elect Israel if they can be saved only by faith in Christ? As long as he is considering the present age, he cannot resolve the dilemma, and finally he solves it by changing categories. 'All Israel will be saved' is not a contradiction of the preceding passage on the olive tree, but the beginning of a new theme, one which transcends the period of human choice and focuses on the boundless mercy of God. 'All Israel' is to be understood along with 'all people' in verse 32 and 'everything' in verse 36. Israel is not singled out for salvation by a separate route, and distinguished from Gentiles, only some of whom are saved; Israel is simply a part of God's final victory, which will embrace the entire creation.

We now see Paul's final theological problem. It is not just that God chose Israel, and that his promise to them might fail. Paul is worried about that, but there is something else. God also created the universe. Will what he created and pronounced good, and especially humanity, created in his own image, ultimately be destroyed? Would that not be the worst failure of all for God, worse than the failure of his promise to Israel?

What, then, is the meaning of the *proclamation of universal redemption* at the end of chapter 11? First let us note that we would have the problem even if we did not have Romans 11. We meet it in Romans 5: 18: 'Then as one man's trespass led to condemnation for all people, so one man's act of righteousness leads to acquittal and life for all people.' This echoes 1 Corinthians 15: 21–2. He does not say 'in Adam all die, but all those in Christ shall be made alive'. The two 'all's are directly parallel. All will live just as much as all die. In 1 Corinthians Paul presses on, saying that first will come 'those who belong to Christ', and then the end. Christ destroys all enemies, finally death, and is then subjected to the Father, 'in order that God may be all in all' (1 Cor. 15: 28). We note the double assertion, that 'those who belong to Christ' rise, but that in the end God takes in 'all things'. We are reminded here of the affirmation that 'all things are from him and through him and unto him' in Romans 11: 36. In this section of 1 Corinthians 15 we have a prediction of the return of the Lord and the end of the world, with no judgement and no condemnation. Christ wins and gives all things over to the Father.

How could Paul, on the one hand, think that it mattered desperately that people come to faith in Christ, say that it determined whether or not they shared Christ's life, and predict destruction for those who rejected his message (for example, Phil. 3: 18–19), and, on the other hand, say that God would save everyone and everything? Which did he really think? Both, almost certainly. But then must it not be the case that he subordinated one to the other: that he thought that finally everyone would come to faith and that thus and only thus would God save them? He might well have thought that had he been a philosophical theologian, concerned to get everything in the right hierarchical relationship to everything else. But he was instead an apostle, an *ad hoc* theologian, a proclaimer, a charismatic who saw visions and spoke in tongues—and a religious genius. Let us not put him entirely into the strait-jacket of logical arrangement.

Paul thought in images and figures. On our topic we can see, or at least glimpse, three. One is the image of the throne conceived as a judgement seat. The second is the image of a race or some other kind of athletic contest. When Paul thought in one of these images, he naturally thought in terms of innocence or guilt and winners or losers. In Philippians 3 we see the image of a contest: he presses on towards the goal (3: 14). He and those who agree with him and, especially, imitate him (3: 17), will win. Others count as enemies of God (here he drops the image of the contest) and will be destroyed (3: 19). The image of the judgement appears in 1 Corinthians 3. 'The day' will come (1 Cor. 3: 13), and everyone's work will be tested. Some will be punished (3: 10–15). Even Paul himself may not be entirely innocent, and he may be punished a bit (4: 4). In this setting he could think that some would be completely condemned, though most of his judgement imagery bears on the relative punishments or rewards of those in Christ (see also 2 Cor. 5: 10). But he doubtless inherited the notion of a judgement which distinguished the wicked from the innocent: it lurks behind Romans 2: 13. This image, even if it remained in the back of his mind, would make it easy for him to discuss the destruction of the wicked.

The third image is that of God as creator and omnipotent king. This is a God who gets his way. He created the world, and he will save all that he created. We see this image very clearly in 1 Corinthians 15 and also in Romans 11: 36 ('from him are all things'). It is this image which takes control in the closing verses of Romans 11.

What would Paul have said if he could have had all this pointed out to him and could have answered? My guess is that he would not retract a point. Of course (he would say) it matters whether or not one becomes part of the body of Christ. Only in that way does one die to sin and live to God. Of course it requires individual commitment. Of course God has chosen some and not others: the elect obtain salvation, the rest are hardened (Rom. 11: 7). Of course God created all people and all things, and he will not lose anything that is his. All of us and all the creation belong to him.

We now see the full consequence of the repeated caution that Paul was not a systematic theologian. He was a theologian: in Romans 9–11, as in Romans 7, he was deeply worried about theological problems. Paul was not systematic, however, since he did not reconcile his responses to these multifaceted problems with one another. We clearly see the deep-seated principles which governed his various answers: God is good and merciful and holds history in his hands; he called Israel and gave the law; he sent Christ to save the world. These underlying assumptions, and the passion with which he applied them, coupled with his bursts of ingenuity and the cut and thrust of his argument, make him a serious and compelling religious thinker. He forces us, in fact, to pose an extremely serious question: must a religion, in addressing diverse problems, offer answers that are completely consistent with one another? Is it not good to have passionate hopes and commitments which cannot all be reduced to a scheme in which they are arranged in a hierarchical relationship?

Notes on Sources

For the Greek text of Paul's letters, I have used the 26th edition of Nestle-Aland, *Novum Testamentum Graece*, though other editions of the Greek New Testament are satisfactory for most purposes. The best English translation, in my view, is the Revised Standard Version (RSV), and I have used it with only minor modifications. At a few points I criticize it, but any translation can be criticized. Other translations referred to are the Jerusalem Bible (JB), the New English Bible (NEB), and the New International Version (NIV).

Most of the quotations from other parts of the Bible are also taken from the RSV. For the Old Testament, the RSV translates the Hebrew text. Paul, however, quoted the Old Testament in Greek translation, which is sometimes different from the Hebrew. His translation was very close to what has come down to us as the Septuagint, and I therefore occasionally note that one of his quotations is from the Septuagint and will not be found in an English translation of the Hebrew. The Septuagint itself may be consulted in a Greek–English edition published by Samuel Bagster and Sons.

The Septuagint included works which were widely read by Greek-speaking Jews and Christians, but which were not accepted in the Hebrew Old Testament. These are now called 'apocryphal' or 'deutero-canonical' books. Of these books, I refer to the Wisdom of Solomon and Tobit. The major English translations of the Bible include them (in Protestant translations they are placed in a separate section).

Two Jewish authors are cited several times: Philo, Paul's older contemporary, who was a leading member of the Jewish community in Alexandria and who wrote extensively on the Bible and the Jewish religion; and Josephus, Paul's younger contemporary, a Palestinian priest who survived the Jewish revolt against Rome (66–73 or 74 BCE). Josephus wrote a history of the revolt (*The Jewish War*), a general account of the history of Israel (*Jewish Antiquities*), an autobiography (*Life*), and a defence of Judaism against its critics (*Against Apion*). The Greek texts of these authors, with English translation on facing pages, are available in the Loeb Classical Library (London and Cambridge, Mass.).

The *Letter of Aristeas* and the *Sibylline Oracles* are classified as 'pseudepigraphical'; translations may be found in *The Old Testament Pseudepigrapha*, 2 vols., ed. James H. Charlesworth (New York, 1983 and 1985).

Some information about Judaism in the time of Paul can be derived from rabbinic literature, a vast body of discussions by Jewish sages. The main collections (the Mishnah, the Tosefta, the Palestinian Talmud, and the Babylonian Talmud) were completed between the third and the sixth centuries CE, but they sometimes include older material. The present work contains only one quotation from rabbinic literature, a passage from tractate Shabbath (on the Sabbath) in the Babylonian Talmud. The English translation is published by the Soncino Press, originally in 35 volumes, now reprinted in 18. Shabbath is in vol. 1.

The *Covenant of Damascus* and the *Community Rule* represent two different wings of the Essene party, one of the pietist groups in first-century Judaism. The best English translation of this sectarian literature is that of Geza Vermes, *The Dead Sea Scrolls in English* (3rd edn., Harmondsworth, 1987).

Ancient authors and scribes did not employ any method of emphasizing words in a sentence; italics in quotations of ancient sources are my own.

Further Reading

Since modern critical scholarship began to be applied to the Bible, Paul has been intensively studied and discussed. Of the older literature, that by Albert Schweitzer is among the most incisive (published in English as *Paul and his Interpreters*, London, 1912; and *The Mysticism of Paul the Apostle*, London, 1931; both often reprinted). Despite Schweitzer's effort to tie the interpretation of Paul to Jewish eschatology, many people continued to view the apostle as being not very Jewish. The book which persuaded most scholars that he must be understood in a thoroughly Jewish context was *Paul and Rabbinic Judaism*, by W. D. Davies (London, 1948; 4th edn., Philadelphia, Pa.,1980).

The present work is primarily dependent on my own two earlier studies, *Paul and Palestinian Judaism* (London and Philadelphia, Pa., 1977) and *Paul, the Law, and the Jewish People* (Philadelphia, Pa., 1983; London, 1985). The former contains a fairly lengthy account of previous scholarship. The most important of the more recent studies are J. Christiaan Beker, *Paul the Apostle* (Philadelphia, Pa., 1980); Wayne A. Meeks, *The First Urban Christians* (New Haven, Conn., 1983); Heikki Räisänen, *Paul and the Law* (2nd edn. Tübingen, 1987; the 1986 edn. published by Fortress Press, Philadelphia, Pa., is easier to obtain and is satisfactory for most purposes).

In Chapter 6 I refer to the influence that Martin Luther has had on the interpretation of Paul. Albert Schweitzer, building on the work of earlier German-speaking scholars, tried to free Paul from Luther's grip. Rudolf Bultmann, unfortunately, re-established it, but he did so with such ingenuity and originality that his work is still interesting to read (published in English as *Theology of the New Testament*, 2 vols., New York, 1951; Paul is discussed in vol. 1). One of the keystones of Bultmann's position—the centrality of 'anthropology' and of Romans 7—was destroyed by Krister Stendahl, in 'The Apostle Paul and the Introspective Conscience of the West', now available in a collection of Stendahl's essays, *Paul among Jews and Gentiles* (Philadelphia, Pa., 1976). The question of Paul and Luther has been especially important in Germany and Switzerland, only slightly less so in the United States. It is primarily scholars from these countries who have pushed Paul back and forth, from being Lutheran to being non-Lutheran, and this subject, often unacknowledged, has been one of the main topics in discussions of Paul's theology.

The French and the British have often stood apart from this contest, and while doing so have written some quite useful explorations of Paul's thought. Especially worthwhile is D. E. H. Whiteley, *The Theology of St. Paul* (Oxford, 1972).

There are several little books on Paul's thought (about the size of the present one). Of these, the best is John Ziesler, *Pauline Christianity* (Oxford, 1983).

Some of the most interesting recent work on Paul, however, falls into the category 'social history' rather than 'theology'. Social history virtually disappeared from New Testament studies after the First World War, to our great loss, since it helps keep scholars' feet on the ground. Still instructive is Adolf Deissmann, *Paul: A Study in Social and Religious History* (2nd English edn., London, 1927; originally published in German, 1911). Wayne Meeks, mentioned above, has led the way back. Also important are Gerd Theissen, *The Social Setting of Pauline Christianity* (Edinburgh, 1982) and Abraham J. Malherbe, *Social Aspects of Early Christianity* (2nd edn., Philadelphia, Pa., 1983). Ronald F. Hock presents a very interesting study of the circumstances of Paul's life in *The Social Context of Paul's Ministry. Tentmaking and Apostleship* (Philadelphia, Pa., 1980).

Paul's life, career and relationships with his churches are the topic of numerous fine studies, among which are Dieter Georgi, *The Opponents of Paul in Second Corinthians* (Philadelphia, Pa., 1986; originally published in German, 1964); John Schütz, *Paul and the Anatomy of Apostolic Authority* (Cambridge, 1975); Bengt Holmberg, *Paul and Power* (Lund, 1978; Philadelphia, Pa., 1980). Pauline chronology has recently been the subject of several major studies, including Robert Jewett, *A Chronology of Paul's Life* (Philadelphia, Pa., 1979); Gerd Lüdemann, *Paul, Apostle to the Gentiles. Studies in Chronology* (Philadelphia, Pa., 1984). Still indispensable, however, is John Knox, *Chapters in a Life of Paul* (Nashville, Tenn., 1950; repr. with new preface, London, 1989). Knox's *Philemon among the Letters of Paul* (2nd edn. Nashville, Tenn., 1959) provides a remarkable insight into Paul the man—charming, resourceful and sometimes manipulative, though in a good cause.

Finally, the world which Paul inhabited: one needs to know the history of the Roman Empire in the first century and its major social and intellectual movements. Then, too, one should know what was going on in Judaism throughout the Mediterranean. The 'social history' books mentioned above provide some help, as do those on Paul and

Judaism. In addition, I shall refer only to a series of eight volumes, the Library of Early Christianity, edited by Wayne Meeks and published by Westminster Press (Louisville, Ky.). The first volume, and one of the best, is *Gods and the One God*, by Robert M. Grant (1986); from there the reader can find the others. They are not uniformly valuable, but they very usefully reveal the scope of the subject. The discussion of Graeco-Roman sexual ethics in Chapter 10 of the present work is primarily dependent on J. K. Dover, *Greek Homosexuality* (London, 1978) and Amy Richlin, *The Garden of Priapus: Sexuality and Aggression in Roman Humor* (New Haven, Conn., 1983). These two books will give the student an idea of the specialist literature that is available on virtually every aspect of the ancient world.

Index

Index compiled by Peva Keane